STE
INTO
MY
WORLD

TRESS CONNOR
&
ALAN CONNOR

JTA PUBLISHING

Thank you to those who gave permission to print testimonials and stories. Certain names have been changed to ensure confidentiality.

BRITISH LIBRARY CATALOGUE IN PUBLICATION DATA
A catalogue record for this book is available from The British Library
ISBN 0 9531878 0 2

First published in Great Britain in 1997.

ACKNOWLEDGEMENTS

From Tress

A big thank you to my guardian angel Leao, who is always by my side, to light, to guard, to guide and to support me. In a similar way, I also thank my grandmother since her passing, for her ever loving, watchful eye throughout my life.

My love and grateful thanks to my husband Joe for his immeasurable love and support in connection with my spiritual work and this book.

A big, big thank you to my son Alan, in helping put this book together (truly a labour of love).

My grateful thanks to all who gave their permission for their stories to appear within the pages of this book.

I would also like to say a big thank you to all of those who have passed on to the higher realms of existence. You have made it possible for this book to be written.

From Alan

Firstly, thank you to my mother for giving me the opportunity to work so closely with her on something so important to her life.

I would also like to thank my father for his support, not only in connection to this book, but throughout my life.

My grandmother, Teresa Hayden, I do miss you terribly but take comfort in knowing that you are never far away. I always know when you're around!

Finally, a big thank you to Bill for proof-reading the book.

Other credits

Photography by Jan Dennis

Drawings by Caroline Tilsle

CONTENTS

INTRODUCTION

Beyond Science

I have been involved in spiritual work for many years now and through every encounter have put to use my analytic mind. I have looked at it from every angle. I have turned it inside out and upside down, in fact, every which way you could possibly think of. I have been a reliable witness for you, the reader. I am on the side of the evidence. I take an oath that everything I am about to tell you is the absolute truth; no lies; no exaggeration; no colouring added. The lady I am writing about (not so much the person, but what comes through her) is one hundred percent genuine. If she were not, I would not be writing this introduction, and Tress would not have written this book.

For what I am about to say later, it may help if I explain a little to you now. When a person makes an appointment to see Tress, the first name only is taken. This is simply for the sake of courtesy. When a person sits down in front of her, they are not allowed to ask any questions. They cannot sit and say "I've come to see you because". This is not permitted. Because it is down to Tress to give them the reason for their visit. If, at the end of the reading, they have anything to ask her then they are free to do so. All of the reading is taped for the person concerned, although there are a couple of exceptions to this rule. The first being when very personal information comes through which, once in a while, a person may not wish to have on tape. The second exception I will discuss later.

It is a hard task to convince people that after death there is life. Perhaps we are too engrossed in our daily lives to give much thought to what may or may not lay beyond our physical existence on Earth. It might be a disturbing thought for some people to consider, perhaps even terrifying. I would hope, however, that after such people have read and digested this book, that the fear will be alleviated and a new confidence and awareness found.

Before you reach the main body of the book, I would like to share with you some of the evidence that I myself have witnessed through one person, that being my wife Tress. She is like two people to me, the person who is my wife and the woman who has this special "gift" (as some would call it) of communicating with those who have passed over. What is this "gift" though and what do we have to support the belief that there is life after death?

Let us assume for a moment that there are people who have the ability to make contact with another dimension; this being a place we all go to when we pass. The name given to a person who has this ability is a medium. Where this name came from I do not know, but what I can tell you is that it is an incorrect term. This is an archaic word which may have been created at a time when our understanding of life after death was infinitesimal to that which it is now. Someday, when it is realised by science that there is at least one other dimension (and possibly more) and they have finally accepted that there are certain people who can make contact with it, the word describing such a person will not be "medium". For now, however, we have to use this term. The evidence you are about to read (if you decide it is

evidence) would indicate that this is the only logical answer and the acceptance of science the best way forward.
I myself have always been on the side of science but there are things happening every day which science say cannot happen. But they are happening. Where science cannot give an answer, common sense can be a great asset. There are scientists who attend church and believe in God. Why would they do that if they do not believe in life after death? If you were to ask one, he may say "I believe in God, but I do not believe a contact can be made with people who have 'died' ". What we have tried to do is show contact is being made with people who have "died" and passed on to another dimension after their life on this earth has ended. The technology to detect this dimension does not yet exist and I personally doubt it ever will. So what science would be dealing with at the moment is invisible, and likely to stay that way. Therefore, it is understandable they appear to have little interest in any of this.
The work of mediums can vary greatly as in any work or profession. Some evidence presented through them can be very poor and its value nil but some can be very good, such as the work I have witnessed regarding Tress. Please remember I am only discussing evidence which has come through one person - that being Tress. I have been a witness to many of the things she has done and I would like to relate some of them to you, concerning evidence for life after this life and evidence that the future is already known to people in this other dimension.
Whether by accident or design, every person on this earth is in fact two people; one being the person you see with your eyes, and the other that which you cannot see, your spirit or soul. When a person "dies", the spirit is released and enters this other dimension (some would call it heaven, others

would call it something else again). Certain people on this earth can make contact with this dimension and the spirit people within it, or to be more precise, it is the spirit people who make the contact with the person on earth.

What would convince you that there is a life after this life? Let us take two people, Jane and John. Both made a pact that whoever died first would come back and make contact with the other using a code word that they had agreed on. Neither knew then if it would be possible. John " dies" first, and over time, Jane starts to think about the code word and how best she might learn if there is life after death. Could you tell her the code word? Could you guess the code word? If you were allowed several thousand words to come up with that one word, do you think you could do it? I do not think Jane would be impressed if you tried it that way.

Jane hears of a genuine medium and decides to see her. She sits down in front of the medium. The first word the medium says to Jane is "Rainbow". Jane starts to cry happy tears, because 'rainbow' is the code word. Accurate information follows. such as John's name and details of how he passed. Then come the names of the family members he is with. Jane is given an abundance of evidence, leaving her in no doubt that it is John supplying the information as he is the only one who could have known all of this.

It is a great comfort to Jane to know that John is still alive albeit in another dimension, and that she will eventually see him again.

Some people might insanely say that when Jane sat in front of the medium, the medium picked from her memory by "mind reading". In a persons brain there are billions of memories. In a billion to one chance, the medium picked the correct word which was the codeword, could you believe this? I do not accept this theory.

Looking for her code word Jane goes to see a medium. She sits down and the medium picks up two pages of writing and starts to read the information to Jane. The first word on the paper is 'rainbow'. The pages of writing are dated fourteen days ago yet Jane made her appointment only three days ago. There goes the mind reading theory, since no contact had been made prior to the time the reading came out and the fact that the medium did not know Jane existed on this earth. I have been a witness to Tress doing readings for people before they have made an appointment, the above has happened many times. This is the second exception to readings being taped.

The first time I saw this in action went like this. A lady phoned on Monday morning to make appointments for three people. I took the call and the address. Tress was to visit the lady's home on the Wednesday night (she does not visit homes anymore). Before this, she was told to sit down and write and she completed the three readings on the Monday night. On the Wednesday night at seven o'clock she arrived at the lady's door and she stepped inside the house. Just then, the phone rang. It was one of the three ladies saying she could not make it but there would be another woman attending in her place. You may think Tress was left with one reading but one of the three readings was for the replacement lady. All the information was correct. These days, she does not often have the time to do readings this way as it involves twice the time of a reading. Once to sit and write it, and once to go through it with the person and put it on tape. Recently, a lady arrived for a reading which had been done this way. She sat down and Tress showed her the pages. The top of page one read "For the lady dressed all in white". To this, the lady replied "today is the first time in my life I have ever dressed all in white". All of the details on the sheets of paper were correct. Information given this way might imply that the future is already known. Let us look at some of the evidence.

Going back some years, I was trying to think of different ways of Tress using her “gift”. If accurate information could be given before a face to face meeting, my thinking was that distance had nothing to do with it; time had nothing to do with it, so if someone is very far away, could she still use this power? It was then I suggested that she should test this theory out over the ’phone, and it worked. Too well! This caused her to spend many hours on the ’phone doing readings for people, often in other countries. There was never a charge for this, other than the person receiving the reading called Tress so that the cost of the call was on their end. Eventually, it got totally out of control and she had to gently put a stop to it. She does, however, occasionally agree to ’phone readings if a person needs urgent help.

Another suggestion I made to Tress was to try and look at the year ahead to see if she could predict any specific events. I am not going to mention all of the items but I would like to elaborate on two of her predictions; one from 1990 and the other from 1991.

In October 1989, one of the predictions for 1990 simply said “M. P.’s will turn against the Prime Minister”. That was all. Then, of course, the Prime Minister was replaced in November that year. The point I am making here is that this information was given to Tress thirteen months before it happened. It was months later we came across the page, quite by accident since these pages had been put to one side and forgotten about. A more serious item came out in 1990, for 1991.

I am not disclosing the persons name. In the 1980’s, a young girl who lived just outside Leeds was abducted and

murdered. The information said the man responsible for the girls' murder would be in custody in 1991. This I remembered and watched for. The year came and went with no mention of this man being in custody. In January 1992, I pointed this out to Tress and told her that the information was wrong. With that, I forgot all about it. Going on my own memory, I think it was February, I read a newspaper report that a man was being questioned about the young girls' murder. In March, a man was charged with both her murder and others. This is where the shock came - he had been in custody since August 1991.
Not all information about future events are given in this way. Sometimes Tress will say to me "I have just seen (such and such a thing) so watch for it". 'Seeing' meaning pictures were being shown to her, usually a short distance in front of her eyes. I would now like to share one of these with you. Usually information received this way precedes the event by about two weeks. We were not to know it at the time, but a major disaster was only twenty- four hours away. In July 1988, once again going by my own memory, we were sitting in the kitchen having a cup of coffee. Tress said to me "I've just seen a mass of tangled wreckage. There is also a group of Scottish pipers. Something is going to blow up around Scotland". That is all I remember being said to me. The next day, an oil rig blew up I watched it on the news. Maybe I was watching more than listing for some reason because I did not link it to anything Tress had said. It was the next day on reading the newspaper that it fell into place on seeing the name in print - "Piper Alpha", the name of the oil rig was Piper Alpha.
Let us look at what Tress said. The mass of tangled wreckage - this was correct. The Scottish pipers was not, so why show her Scottish pipers? It is quite obvious. It was a clue to the

name. Just suppose we had known oil rigs had names and we checked to see if there was a rig with the name 'Piper' and we were told there is a rig called 'Piper Alpha' and I informed them my wife is a medium and she has seen an oil rig blow up with the name Piper. If he did not hang up the phone straight away and he asked "when?" I would have replied "Maybe inside the next two weeks." Who could blame the man for thinking he was talking to a crazy person? But suppose Tress's information gave the exact day, and the man on the phone said we will check the rig out, so they check it out and everything is fine. Five minutes later, the accident happens. Two points to make here. The information was nowhere near enough to do anything with it, plus you can't stop it happening. If something is meant to happen, it's going to happen, but if a person working on the rig had been to see Tress the day before then it is very likely the person would have received a warning. The fact is Scottish pipers had nothing to do with it. Asking the next question can create the pebble in the pond effect or "ripples". Each "ripple" creating another question. Could the evidence be stronger because Scottish pipers was wrong? Can you imagine the scene. Someone is trying to decide how to give the name piper in picture form, (why?) and decides on Scottish pipers, does it show evidence of outside intelligence?
Evidence has shown an individual may be helped but you can't stop the disaster. So why show her these pictures at all? The only purpose it seems to serve is to show the future exists. So, a person may be given limited helpful advice about their future, but the evidence may show the earth itself is included. It may have its own future, or at least what happens on the earth, like "disasters". Could this be a small part of the answer to the question "why are we here"? Does

it show there is a purpose? If so, it may imply we are all part of a plan, and this plan extends into another dimension. It does not make sense to "kill us all off", and death be final. Could a "plan" indicate we have to "experience" suffering? Would an outside intelligence not look upon it as "suffering" but as "learning"? Why is it some people suffer (learn) more than others? Could there be a reason which is not realised until the person "dies"? The only part of this I simply cannot understand is that the future exists. It has to be a give and take affair rather like a winding road and it can change from time to time. The reason I say this is because in a reading with Tress a person may be given advice on how to avoid bad situations (if it was in a person's future to be in a bad situation) yet they are allowed advice which if followed will change that future. The future has to some extent to be changeable. The evidence is there but the 'how's' and 'why's' of it, like who decides the future and where is the information stored I do not know. I cannot comprehend it.

I would like to tell you about a healing I watched take place some years ago. Tress had a problem with her hip and leg. She had no feeling in the back of her leg and; it was like her leg was constantly asleep and dead. She would have to get up in the middle of the night and rub her leg to try and get some life in it. There was also a lot of pain connected with this problem which was the result of a trapped nerve, thought to be in the hip. She was on very strong pain killers and was taking them for quite a number of years. Eventually, her doctor sent her to see a specialist. After examining her hip and leg his advice was when she could bear the pain no longer a major operation would be necessary. This was not good news. As time went on and the pain got worse, Tress said to me one day "you should try and help me with some healing on my leg". This to me was very funny as I did not

do anything like that. I assumed she was having a little joke but as it turned out she was very serious.
She asked several times over the days and in the end I gave in. Feeling a little foolish, I sat at one end of the settee and Tress sat at the other. She placed the problem leg across my knees and I then only did as she directed me. I was instructed first to concentrate, then place one hand on the sole of her bare foot and the other hand just above her knee. After a few minutes, I saw with my own eyes a small wave effect take place in the area between her knee and her ankle. Seeing it broke my concentration, but the movement still continued. I could not believe what I was seeing. She was not moving her toes or her leg yet the movement was there. After twenty minutes, Tress said I could stop. Before she stood up I asked her to move her toes, to see what kind of movement it caused in her leg, it was not the same and there was no comparison. Tress stood up and her leg was fine. There was no more pain or any more need to take pain killers and to this day that problem has never returned.
The number of people Tress has helped to heal goes into the thousands. She has never accepted payment for it. As to what is happening when healing takes place, I myself have never felt a thing, though it would appear some kind of energy is going into the person receiving the healing. They sometimes feel heat. What is it "made" of? How does it "heal"? Where does this energy come from? Twice it has been said to me by people watching a friend having healing from Tress they have seen a "purple glow" between Tress's hands and the person receiving healing.
One time in Leeds market I was buying some writing paper I knew the gentleman in the shop because I often went there for odds and ends. On this occasion after visiting his shop I arrived home and Tress was there. She handed me a cup of

coffee. We were both sitting and talking when I remember her eyes looking to my right, then looking at me, then looking again to my right. I said to her "I'd bought some shopping in the market".

Tress asked "who were you talking to in the market?"

I replied "no one really, just some small talk with the man in the shop. Why'd you ask?"

"Because", she said, "his mother is standing beside you."

I of course, could not see a thing. This is why she had been glancing to my right. How might this be so? I was making small talk with the man in the shop. Unknown to me his mother was beside him looking at me. She must have somehow seen my wife was a medium. This gentleman's mother appears to have followed me all around town and came home with me, just so she could ask Tress to pass on information to her son. The lady gave Tress quite a lot of information, in fact it came very fast, so fast I had to take over the writing with Tress telling me what to put down. The lady asked Tress to make sure that her son received the information. She thanked Tress and left. The next day, Tress went to see the man in the shop and gave him the information, which he read. He could relate to ninety-eight per cent of it. The remaining two per cent was apparently concerning the future.

I was not around when this next item happened. Tress told me about it. She was walking through Leeds city centre, when a gypsy lady stopped and asked her to buy something and she would tell Tress her fortune. She gave the lady some money and said "never mind telling me anything, but I have someone here for you. You lost your son in a motor cycle accident a few months ago." When Tress had finished passing on the information, the gypsy lady laid her head on Tress's shoulder and wept. Again I have to say these were

happy tears. I have always liked that story.
I never forget that Tress knew her uncle had passed before anyone on this earth told her. Her uncle told her himself. I was a witness to this. Two days after she was told, she received a letter from her mother, telling her of his passing. How can you explain that, other than there is a life after death?
There is evidence that there are several levels in this other dimension, and our behaviour on this earth may determine how pleasant or unpleasant the level we go to is when we pass on. The spiritual message Tress tries to pass on, is that people should care about people; help rather than hurt. In the long run you could be helping yourself. None of us can be perfect, but if we try and be a little decent as we go through life, when our last minutes on this earth arrive I do not think we would have much to worry about. Being involved in this brings no special favours, we get the same knocks and problems as everyone else. In Tress's work there are rules. If you consider this, a child starts to attend school and during the child's school years you may from time to time help the child with school work, but you do not give all the answers, otherwise the child would not learn very much. This is why concerning the future, a little is told, but by no means everything. Even Tress's guides are governed by laws higher than themselves.
To tell you the following story, I had to get in touch with the mother involved to check the facts, but they are as I remember them. I am only trying to make a point, so I am only giving a skeleton version of it. I prefer not to mention names of people, hospitals, or the disease. A mother gives birth and there appears to be something wrong with the baby. Shortly after, the hospital's opinion is that the baby has a rare disease. The mother knew Tress and trusted her. She

took the baby to Tress who told the mother "your baby does not have this disease". She was advised by Tress to have a second opinion. This she eventually did but the second opinion also said that the baby had the disease. The mother informed Tress of this and Tress said to her "I stand by what I said. They are mistaken. You have to get another opinion." This took many months to achieve. When it was arranged the baby went through many, many tests over many weeks. More tests were performed over time, more than at any other time. Add to this the people involved knew exactly what they were looking for. The results of the tests were the baby did not have the disease although they could see why someone else may have thought so. The point being, what made Tress say the baby did not have the disease? She is not a doctor, where did the accurate information come from? During all of this the baby was receiving healing from Tress.

As I am almost finished with this introduction, let me say Tress Connor is a spiritual medium working on a spiritual level for the common good - she tries to help. A problem Tress faces is she is only one person and cannot do as much as she would like to do. I can't tell you the countless people she has helped. Her information has even prevented people committing suicide, how can people find fault with that?

All over the world people have various beliefs. That's fine, so long as that belief does not impinge on another persons free will. If any belief interferes with a persons free will there is something wrong. We all come in to this world the same way, we all leave this world the same way, if a person thinks because what they believe means they go to a different place than someone with a different belief, there is no evidence to support that. Only a persons behaviour on this earth may alter the level they go to. When one has a bereavement, be it family or friend, this information may or may not be of immediate help since the grief is too great. As time passes it may be a comfort. If a person is aware their time on this earth is nearly over - presuming they believe the information it will be a definite help. If they have the information, even if they do not believe it, it will still be a help because as they pass on they instantly know it is true. There is evidence for a very short time, be it minutes or seconds, before the final breath is taken a person may already be seeing spirit family or friends from this other dimension.

The evidence I have described does not even scratch the surface.

There is nothing in what I have said I would term a miracle, but I am going to show you a miracle, a real miracle. Look in a mirror, that's a miracle - YOU, a miracle of creation. As this life nears its end, please remember

The Best Is Yet To Come.

1

My Early Years

After the Second World War ended and the minions were recovering from years of anguish and turmoil, Ireland had its fair share of celebrations. People took great joy in taking down the air raid shelters from the cobbled streets and welcoming loved ones back from England where many of the country's men had served in the army.

I was born in the heart of Dublin in that early spring. It was 2.45 am when I was handed into my mothers arms for the first time My mother, Teresa Hayden, gave birth to me just across the road from where my family (which at that time consisted of my father Jack and older brother Joseph) lived, at the Coombe Maternity Hospital. This was one of two dedicated maternity hospitals in Dublin and half the city's children were born here.

The house I lived in for the first ten years of my life was situated on one of the busiest streets in Dublin. It was one of the tenement terraced houses which were split up into private flats. Ours was a nice area with friendly people who would lean out of their windows chatting to each other and exchange pleasantries with passers-by on the streets below. Children were always safe to play on our street as there was always a protective eye on them.

The house we lived in was split into two flats. Ours was

located on the second floor and consisted of two large rooms. Our bedroom was at the front and two large windows brightened it at night as the street lights shone through. The second room, across the landing, was the living area. It had a sink in one corner next to the back window. Across at the other side was a very old sideboard, on top of this was an enamel basin with a big jug standing in the middle of it. In the centre of the sideboard was a radio, which, since we had no electricity as the flat was not wired up, had no interior workings and was just a shell. I presume it was kept there for appearances sakes. Further down along the wall was an old Corporation (or council) gas cooker. It was black and heavy looking and was usually installed in the homes of those of "limited means". Nearby was the open fireplace which was always warm and cosy looking and a joy to sit in front of and make toast!

There was another window, which was behind the door on the left. It was a very unusual window because it actually looked down onto the stairs leading up from the front door! It was presumably used to let more light into the living room and to identify whose footsteps were coming up the stairs! We ate at a table underneath this window and sat there a lot. My mother sawed the legs off an old chair and I would stand on this at the table to eat my meals, which were always hearty. Afterwards mum would engage in an almost ritual scrub down of the whole table.

We all shared the bedroom. My mother's bed was against the wall behind the door, whilst my brother slept across the other side of the room beneath the window. I slept in my cot which was in front of (although away from) the fireplace. It was in this cot that I had my first psychic experiences.

My mother told me that as soon as I could stand up in my cot, I would quite happily chat away to myself, often well into the small hours, instead of lying down and going to sleep. It soon became apparent to her that there was something more going on than just the babbling of a small child - I was actually having a conversation with someone. She once described to me how I would heartily chat away to thin air, pausing occasionally as if listening to a reply. She could of course only hear what I was saying but admitted to me that she could feel a very strong presence within the room, which was obviously the focal point of my attentions. Our room was lit by a small gaslight which was expensive to run, but whenever my mother tried to extinguish the flame I would scream and cry as I was nowhere near ready to go to sleep! So for the sake of the others in the room and some peace and quiet, mum took to buying a very large candle which she stuck into a hollowed out swede. She put this on the table next to her bed which was out of my reach, but it gave me enough light to continue my "conversations". My mother never showed concern over my chats as she said they were always quite lively and I seemed to be happy so she knew I was safe. Quite often I would put my arms out through the bars of my cot as if to give someone a big hug! On occasion she noted that I would suddenly stop talking and seemed to go to sleep in an instant or "dead to the world" as she would say. I would flop down in a heap, she would then get up, lift me and put me under the covers, extinguish my light and retire for the night herself.

If I was alert and energetic at night when I should have settled down to sleep, I'm sure you can imagine what I was like during the day. For as long as I can remember I could not stay put in one place for long unless I was talking to someone interesting, which is probably why my mother deemed it appropriate to put me on a harness whenever we went out or when I was sat at the bottom doorway which lead out onto the busy Coombe Street. She would attach a piece of string to the reins to give me a little mobility and the freedom to walk to the hall door but no further. I could then sit at the doorway and chat to people going by. She would tie this string to a hook on the wall above the stairs high up on the wall so I could not reach it. She could then continue with her daily routine leaving me to my own amusement, and occasionally check on me through the large window that overlooked the stairs.

One day I somehow managed to break free from my reins, and to this day my mother does not know how it happened, as I was far too small to reach the hook. She has often said it was like I was "spirited away", meaning one minute I was there and the next I was gone! Luckily I was found...four miles away and hours later up at the Harold Cross cemetery. A lady and her husband saw me on my own outside the cemetery gates with an old bus ticket in my hand. The lady became concerned about me because I was so young and I appeared to be alone. She bent over me and asked me where my mother was to which I replied "she's at home on the Coombe". The lady remained with me whilst her husband went away to look around the cemetery to make sure that I wasn't there with a visitor paying their respects.

After establishing that this was not the case, they brought me back to the Coombe, which was a well known area because of the hospital, and returned me to my mother's arms, who by this time was frantic with worry, whilst I was as cool as a cucumber. The lady told my mother that I was perfectly happy and had been chatting away as if to an imaginary friend, seemingly not disturbed by the fact that I had been lost. Everyone had expected me to be crying and screaming and running about looking for my mother!

I do have a vague recollection of this day as I had a dirty old bus ticket in my hand, although I don't know where it came from or even how I got up there. I myself think that it was an unusual place for a child to be found but I do strongly believe that I was not intended to come to any harm as there were far worse places I could have ended up. I know for certain that my imaginary friend whom I had been seen talking to would not have let me come to any danger because I now know he was not imaginary at all, and is indeed, a real friend.

****

As a child, I used to have difficulty getting off to sleep, even when I wasn't engaged in conversation with the other side. However, I recall one particular night quite vividly because I was unusually distressed about it. I could hear a very loud ticking, rather like that of a clock and no matter how I tried I could not block it out. Also, the more I tried to ignore it the louder it got. I remember calling over to my mother and asking if I could sleep in her bed with her as there was a noise coming through the wall. My mother protested insisting that it was nothing but eventually she gave in. The ticking then subsided.

Just as I was beginning to feel secure it started again - only this time louder than before. I woke my mother again and asked if she could hear it. I pleaded with her to listen and kept saying that "Time is running out". By then mum had woken up and looking at me replied "Please don't tell me that child". I felt better when I had said this and that I had been heard, so I settled down to sleep and thought no more about it or the ticking from the wall.

Within a few days, mother received a telegram saying that grandma was very ill and she should come home straight away. She immediately arranged for us all to be looked after and set off for County Westmeath which is a good way from Dublin. My mother recalled to me how, whilst at my grandmother's bedside, she had said to granddad that she could see Jesus with his arms stretched out towards her and he was bathed in a brilliant light. Grandma had always gone to 6 o'clock mass on Sundays and, not wanting this day to be any different, had got dressed to go. She had only gone a few yards when she collapsed from a stroke. Two more strokes followed through the course of the evening. She opened her eyes for the last time in the early hours of Monday morning to say goodbye to the family and was gone. My grandma was a wonderful, deeply spiritual lady who was dearly loved by all. She had a little prayer corner in her bedroom and I have been told that she was always in her room saying a prayer for someone, which is of no surprise to me as both she and my grandfather were healers. The gift is long running in my family.

When it was time for my grandfather to leave this world, which was many years later, he told his family his wife was with him. Mother told me he had the most beautiful smile on his face as she was sitting holding his hand when he died. My grandparents were a very united couple and after grandma died, my grandfather never slept in their bedroom again as she was not beside him. He very much looked forward to, and welcomed the day when they would stand together again. They both have guided me through time and still heal, although now it is in spirit.

My love of the company of old people has always been strong. It extended beyond that of my grandparents to those who lived in the more immediate area of the Coombe. Often, when I was not much older than three, I would talk to these people, who were like guardian angels to me. They would watch me from their windows and should I happen to talk to anyone they deemed would have a bad influence on me, would call me to come and sit with them. They would promptly call me a good girl and tell me to stay away from that person.

My mother once took the trouble to find out why these people were so interested in talking to me and one day listened to our conversations. She heard me telling one woman not to visit her friend today as she would not be in and I told another not to go up to the Murphys pub yet as it was closed, but to wait ten minutes because the landlord would then be back! My mother thought it was hilarious that half the street should take notice of the advice of such a small child but as one of the women was quick to point out on the occasions when she had not heeded my words and had gone to her friends, she had indeed been out.

You may at this point get the impression that I had no time for anyone of my own age. This is not true. I had a great many young friends and I was especially fond of a girl called Josie. She was sitting with me one day, it was approaching Easter, and we were swapping silver coloured wrapping paper. It made me think of Easter eggs, which I had a great fondness for, and I remember talking about them. Josie could be quite vindictive at times and on this occasion quite cruelly said to me "You have nothing, you never get any nice things, I bet you won't even get an Easter egg on Easter Sunday, and you never have anything new."

This comment caused me to turn on her, and without taking a breath and my finger pointing at her I retorted, "One day I am going to have a house of my own, and I mean MY own, I'll have a wonderful family and everything I want. I'll have a colour television, a telephone and lovely furniture and a garden and you'll be sleeping on your mother's floor, with a young baby in your arms with nowhere to go and married to a brute for a husband". Then I stopped. I suddenly realised that I had no control over this flowing emotional outburst. I was frightened but the feeling quickly subsided as I could somehow sense that these words were being given to me by some source I could not understand. It was a force though, that I had always had with me.

This certainly was the beginning for me of being aware that I could see things in this way. It also amuses me to this day how I saw colour televisions when they hadn't even been invented then! Later, when I had spoken with my grandmother who was in spirit and had been behind me at the time of my outburst I was warned that I would have to keep my mouth shut or I would end up in a lot of trouble.

Years later everything I had predicted on that day had happened - it was sad for Josie, and my account of it all was very accurate. Josie, however was wrong and I did get an Easter egg from my father - a great big one that you had to use a hammer on to crack the chocolate!

It is sad to say though that what Josie said was largely right most of the time and getting something as grand as an Easter egg was very rare. That is not to say that we were neglected. My father was away a lot on business and my mother worked practically every hour God sent to keep us.

One day near Easter, a little while before my outburst at Josie, my brother was supposed to be keeping an eye on me, as my mother had just got a job doing some shop work. We were walking towards some old waste ground, so that my brother could rummage around. To get to it, there was a road to cross, but my brother did not want me to get dirty as my mother would be angry, so he told me to wait on this side for him as he ran across the road. I on the other hand, loved to get dirty! I could hear a horse and cart coming down the road, but I thought it was far enough away for me to make it if I made a dash too. My brother shouted at me to stay where I was but I was convinced I would make it, so I ran. To my horror I tripped and landed face down in the middle of the road. I noticed that the driver of the cart had seen me because he was weaving across the road trying to get the horse to stop. He lost control of his speed as he came towards me and I panicked. I stared at the cart as it came hurtling towards me and I could clearly see the rims of the wheels a fraction away from my fingers and feel the horse standing over me. I heard the driver roaring at me not to move so as not to frighten the horse, who could have trampled me to death. I was terrified and needless to say, at such a young age I didn't take any notice of him. Then suddenly, I felt like I had been sucked out of the back of my body with an almighty whoosh. I remember it so vividly, it was the strangest experience I had yet had. I was aware that I was standing with my grandmother (who I now know to be one of my spirit guides), and I could hear a voice saying "OK". I could hear other things but they were quieter, less vivid. I was actually looking at myself lying in the middle of the road with the man from the cart standing over me.

I now know of course that this was my first out of body experience. I was confused about it at the time as I did not know what to make of the sensation of having been torn from my body. When I came around a little, I noticed my left arm looked strange - it had broken out in red spots, measles I thought, but it seemed not, as the doctors later could not explain it. Whilst my poor mother was working herself up into a terrible state asking if I would be all right I just seemed to shrug it off. I somehow knew that it was necessary for me to live. I knew I had something important to do and I was being kept safe. In fact, all I was concerned about after it all was whether or not my mother would buy me a marshmallow Easter egg!

2

Growing Up

My mother had another daughter after me who was called Clare. We were very close, literally, because we both had to sleep in my cot! I didn't like sharing the cot because she would be lying on my hair all night and my hair was very long. Also, since I was about five, I had really outgrown this particular kind of bed. Mother couldn't spare the money to buy me a new bed, but because she did not want to see me disappointed, she decided to build me one herself. I recall watching her sawing down and sanding pieces of wood and hammering them together to make the frame. My mother was very creative when she had to be! She asked me what colour I would like my bed to be. "Blue!" I replied, and so it was painted. She had to sew the material together to make a mattress but I didn't care how makeshift it was, because at last I had my own proper bed.

Clare wasn't the only new arrival to the Hayden household. My mother then went on to have a baby boy. We were so near to the maternity hospital, as I've already detailed earlier, that my mother wasn't admitted when she was giving birth to my brother, he was instead born at home when I was five years old. When the doctor came to the flat to deliver the baby, my sister and I were placed in the back room out of the way. We had to sleep on a mattress on the floor in there for two days. I was puzzled as to why all this was going on, but it became clear to me later in the evening when I heard a baby crying across the hall. I couldn't ask my older brother because he was staying at a neighbour's for the night and my father wasn't around either. He'd spent some time in the British army and he may have been at base or else he was away working. You had to go where the work was in those days as, after the war, it was hard to come by.

Shortly after I noticed the crying, my aunt came into the room holding the baby in her arms and informed us that this was our baby brother, Seamus. Mother had insisted that he be shown to us so that we could welcome him into the world with a kiss on the forehead. We were told not to touch the top of his head though as the skin was thin around there. I was so carried away in the moment that I gave him two kisses, an extra one for luck and from that day on I said I would help look after him. In the years that followed he would often come to me with his troubles. Finally though, my mother's family was now complete. It was probably just as well as there was hardly any room left in the bedroom!

As I grew older I began to be much more aware of my connection with the spirit plain, although I did not really perceive it in the same way as today. I began to feel that there was something more to these voices, something that most other people were unaware of, and I put my complete trust in them. It is probably just as well as I would more than likely have joined them by now had I not heeded their words. There was one instance, not long after the birth of my brother, when I was on my way to school. I was walking down the stairs of the flat and I turned back to say goodbye to my mother. I was just about to put my foot on the third step from the bottom when I heard an unfamiliar but authoritative voice shout "Jump now". I didn't think twice about it and leapt immediately. Just as I did the whole ceiling came crashing down around the steps I had been standing on, only just missing me. The landlord had been repairing the roof a few days before and had left the old roof tiles underneath the new ones. Their weight had, of course, brought down the plaster. Once again spirit had come to the rescue.

****

It is customary in Ireland for catholic children to take part in two religious ceremonies as they grow up. The first of these, at around age six, is Communion. My first communion was to be a very grand day for me as I was to have all new clothes for the occasion. New clothes were important to me as we did not get store bought clothes very often. As I have established, mother worked hard to keep us and although my father worked away a lot; we saw very little income from him to the household. Most of our clothes were bought second hand from the market and cut down to size to fit us. On this special occasion though I looked like a little princess. I was wearing a beautiful button up dress with a bow at the back, a gift from my Godmother (who was my aunt) from America. I also wore patent shoes and a cherry red coat that my mother had made. It was a wonderful day. It also marked the day when I was told that I would have to contribute more to the finances of our home. There was heating to provide and food to be put on the table, and life would be better for all if we all helped out.
I never minded pitching in to help my family. I had always been accustomed to hard work and never took anything for granted. My job was to sell firewood. I had to collect things like empty fruit boxes and break up the wood to sell around

the neighbourhood. Needless to say, since I was not the most fashionably dressed or typical child around, I was left open to a lot of abuse about my lifestyle and my family. I learned to live with the taunts from malicious children about us. They would say things like "Go home pauper" and make fun of my clothes. All this only served to make me a stronger person and I felt their shame at these remarks in years to come. I would just hold my head up and smile. Those times in my life made me strong and I learned what it was like to survive in the face of adversity. I am grateful for these experiences now because they moulded me and prepared me for the times when I would have to help someone realise that no matter what, you can and do get over the problems in your life and beat the obstacles. I know though, that in order to preach you must have experienced, and I had plenty such experiences growing up.

You may be wondering how my father could have let us exist like this. Let me tell you a blunt and straightforward fact about him. He could not keep hold of his money. It was as simple as that. He did not drink, although he spent a lot of time in the pub, that was simply because he liked attention and talking to people. He had been spoiled as a child as he was the baby of his family. In a lot of ways he never really grew up. My mother's family were quite comfortably off and had given my parents a good start in married life by setting them up with a bed and breakfast business. It didn't take long before my fathers extravagant lifestyle cost them this. My grandfather helped them out again, this time by buying them a shop. My father constantly gave away shop goods for free to all the ladies in the area and to any man who complemented him. Still my mother stayed with him because she loved him. After his third intervention, my grandfather warned that he would help them no more as there were other children in the family who were going to be deprived, and so his last gesture was to buy them a coal wagon. This too was lost. My father's parents were not so generous as they knew all about Jacks inability to hang on to his money. I do not hate or think badly of my father for all this. It is simply the way he was. He passed away some time ago and one thing that I have learned you must never do is hold ill will against someone, especially those in spirit, as it holds them back.

So we became accustomed to my father not being around and managing as best we could. I never went without the necessities as you now know, my mother would do everything within her power to accommodate my needs, as with my bed.

To me, that bed has always been very special, partly because it was such a blessing to have and my mother had worked hard to make it, and partly because it was also the sight of my second out of body experience. It happened late one night. I'd been listening to the sound of the buses going past our house and was just closing my eyes to go to sleep. The light from the street light outside used to shine in and illuminate the corner of my room. Everything was as it would normally have been. I suddenly became aware that everything had gone deathly quiet and so I opened my eyes to see what had happened. At least I thought I'd opened my eyes but I could see nothing, no bedroom, no light, just emptiness.

I then realised that I was someplace else, floating in the narrow gap between the ceiling and the tiles of the roof. I was aware of a tremendous feeling of peace like I had never felt before. Suddenly, the roof disappeared from above and I was ascending upwards to the stars. I could not understand what was happening. As soon as I had begun to think about this strange experience I found myself back in my room and within my body. It was years later that I realised this was an out of body experience (hereafter o.b.e.) and it was to be the landmark event of the many that followed in the course of my life.

Another such landmark, although much more distressing, was just around the corner.

It was the day after my confirmation, the second of Ireland's traditional religious ceremonies, which had taken place on the 8th of March 1957. I remember it all so well because there were so many exciting things going on at the time. It was the year of rock and roll; or the year of Bill Haley to be a little more exact. He had just taken the world by storm with a single called "Rock around the clock". The song was also the title and inspiration for a new film which was revolutionising the music industry. Large crowds of teenagers were descending upon small, unsuspecting cinemas that were showing the film and tearing them apart. These youths or "teddy boys" as they had begun to be called, were causing chaos and creating new guidelines for teenagers of the future. Times were definitely changing - and I was loving every minute of it.

On the day after my confirmation, the rock 'n' roll bug was in full 'swing' and teddy boys were everywhere, more often than not on the way to the cinema. I remember passing some of them on the street this particular day. It was quite a normal day, mother was looking after a neighbour's dog and was busily making dinner. My friend Josie was with me and we must have been getting under my mother's feet because she sent us out to play for a while. We decided to walk a short distance to Ash Street and play there, with the intention of returning later for our food. On the way, we were delayed somewhat by a neighbour who wanted us to relay a message to a friend, and so, after our good deed, we were left with little time to play and started to walk home. In the distance we could see black smoke billowing over the rooftops. I just knew it was our home. When I told Josie this she looked at me as if I was demented and told me not to be silly, but I insisted and so we ran the rest of the way.

I was right. The flames were leaping from our building and the fire department was already there battling frantically to get the fire under control. There was of course the very real danger that the fire would spread across the terraced roofs destroying other homes.

I was distraught. Not because my every possession was being burnt to a cinder in front of my eyes, but because I knew my mother was still in there. I started yelling "My Mum's in there. Somebody help her!" Neighbours and friends were saying everything would be okay and that everyone had been removed from the building. "No" I cried, "she's still in there". Eventually a stranger had the good sense to take note of what I was saying and, removing his handkerchief and putting it over his mouth, he ran into the building. He emerged shortly after, after a futile attempt to get up the stairs to our flat but he announced that it was impossible. He began shouting for someone to bring a ladder. By now the crowds that had gathered were all murmuring that if anyone was still in there then they would surely be dead.

I didn't believe that for an instant and rushed to the back of the building. When I got there I could see my mother, clutching the dog, standing on a platform underneath the back room window. She was being held by my older brother as if to stop her from jumping the great height down. It was probably a very tempting idea for them as the thick smoke was flowing from the window above like water over Niagara Falls.

A clutch of minutes later and my mother and brother were brought safely down on a ladder. It seemed that my mother had been trying to open the window herself, but whilst grappling with the stiff latches had lost her balance and fallen backwards, knocking herself unconscious on our sewing machine. Luckily for her my older brother had found her in time and pulled her through the window himself.

By now, reporters and photographers were everywhere. We all had our photos taken and were then promptly ushered towards a waiting ambulance. As we walked, I caught sight of some teddy boys who were standing on the hoses the firemen were using so as to stop the supply of water. I quickly shot one of them a glaring look and he moved away, pulling the others with him. To this day, it still amazes me how some people can find it so amusing to watch someone's home go up in smoke like that.

At the hospital, we were all checked over for shock and my mother and brother were treated for smoke inhalation. We were very lucky that no one was killed. When the morning newspaper came out we had made the front page. We were stars! It was, however, a very costly fifteen minutes of fame.

The fire took three-and-a-half hours to extinguish. Thankfully, no other buildings were destroyed. The cause of the fire still remains a mystery although it is known that it was not started in our flat as the fire had spread from the ground floor upwards.

****

Our new flat was only a few years old and was very modern. We considered anything that was wired for electricity very modern! It was part of a three story block known as St. Teresas Gardens. We were, once again, on the top floor but this time there were two bedrooms, a living room, separate kitchen and indoor bathroom. The only thing we did not now have was furniture. Starting again from scratch was not easy and we had to make do with orange boxes to sit on and an old billy can to make tea in for a while. Our saviours turned out to be the Salvation Army and Red Cross who gave us bedding and furniture with which to build our home again. Everything was going well until I discovered that there was a problem.

I had to avoid the front bedroom, there was a feeling, a sense of something quite nauseous that I was disgusted by. If I stood in the room for any length of time, I could feel my skin begin to crawl. I was not happy about it, but this was our new home and I had to make the best of things but I knew I would be avoiding that room as much as possible. When mother asked us all which bedroom we would like to sleep in, I gave no one a chance to speak and asked for the back room. I decided not to alert anyone else in the family to my fears as I felt that we had all been through enough in the last week, it would be my secret, for now anyway.

As time went by, I had little cause to use the room, in fact the only time I ever went near it was when I had to use the mirror in there. We only had one mirror and it was so big that the only place we could put it was on top of the dresser in that room. I hated looking in it though as I would often see what looked like mist forming behind me. The room often looked like someone had smoked an entire packet of cigarettes and left the window closed, such was the effect. It got me so scared that I wouldn't even close the door when I was in there.

Everyone else was very happy with the room and never passed comment about it, or so I thought. One day relatives from America were over visiting and decided to spend time with us before going down to the rest of the family in Westmeath. Mother announced that they would be sleeping in my room and I would have to move into the front bedroom. My only consolation was that mum and Clare would be in there with me, with my brothers pushed out onto the living room floor. It had been a very hectic day and my mother had laid awake most of the first night talking about how exciting it was to see her family again but eventually we said "Goodnight" and settled down to sleep. No matter how hard I tried though, I could not let myself go because I was so aware of the presence in the room. I noticed that my mother was restless too and so I spoke to her. "I know you can't sleep either because you know we are not alone here". Mother let out a little sigh of relief and whispered, "So you can feel it too. How long have you known?" I quickly explained how I'd known from the moment I had first set foot in there. My mother was quite frightened by it all and we both stayed awake all night as she simply could not bring herself to sleep. The next day she dowsed the room in holy water for protection. I did not have the heart to tell her that it would do little good. This room had a heart and soul of its own and nothing would remove the life from it. The room even had a history in the brief time it had been standing. The previous occupants of the flat had not stayed long because they could not take to it and had had some kind of "experience" there. I was to have one of my own in that room myself in time to come.

Apart from the room, however, everything was working out fine. My older brother was working and mum was as busy as always. Clare was doing well and so was my wonderful young brother. I still missed our old street though and often returned there to see my friends, especially Josie. One particular day we were playing with another friend of ours,

Liz, who went to the same school as us. Liz had a wonderful voice and was proud of showing it off. She often had an audience as the women on the street would stand and listen to her. One of these women in particular intrigued me. She was a young married woman who lived across the road from Liz. She had been married several years but had no children, which is very unusual for an Irish family as there are usually children everywhere. We all knew that married ladies ended up with large tummies and when they came out of hospital their large tummies would be gone and they would have a baby. We also knew that nuns never had children because they weren't married (except to God). I often smile at this now, but at the time the facts of life were not spoken about. Eventually I learned that this woman was waiting to adopt a baby and when I heard of this I told everyone that when she had got this baby in her arms, her own would follow. Unsurprisingly, people thought this was highly amusing and paid little attention to it, labelling me as foolish. When the day came that the lady did have her adopted baby, I told her my prophecy. She wasted no time in telling me to mind my own business and that I didn't know what I was talking about. I, however, had the last laugh when the obvious signs of my prediction became apparent. When the baby was born my friends never questioned my words again, and the woman who had spoken harshly to me that day could never bring herself to look me in the eye again. Out of the mouth of babes can come many words of truth and wisdom, I say.

3

Teenage Life

The time between my confirmation and fourteenth year of life was spent mostly on working hard to pass school exams and rebuilding our home life. Things were changing for us. My older brother had got a job in a steel works and so was contributing quite a lot of money to the family and for the first time in my life I found that we were in possession of a record player and radio (one that actually had the insides in!)

Within this period my character was also developing. I am not the shy retiring type and I've always spoken my mind. This seemed to be becoming much more of the case as I got older as my gift was getting stronger. In retrospect, when I think of some of the things I have said to people, I am lucky to have made twenty! I have never liked it when people spoke ill of someone behind their back and continue to this day to defend those who are not always there to defend themselves. Some of my friends often got the sharp side of my tongue when I was at this point in my life. For example, shortly before my fourteenth birthday I had fractured my ankle whilst running from a bull in a field (that's another story!) I subsequently found myself hobbling along on crutches. An acquaintance of mine, Margaret, wanted to play with them as she had never had crutches before. I did not like the idea and warned her that if she did this then she would be on crutches herself within the week. She laughed at this and took the crutches from the side of the chair where I was sitting and waddled around on them for awhile. About a week later I saw Margaret again only this time on crutches! She had fallen down the stairs the previous day and broke her leg. So there we were, two friends on crutches together!

At the time all this was transpiring, I was studying for my Irish Leaving Certificate (which was the equivalent to GCSE's). I still feel cheated to this day as I did not get my certificate, failing on the Gaelic test by just one point. I think that it was a very unfair way of assessing a candidates abilities as I attained a pass mark in all my other subjects. Certainly the British test system is much fairer as you are graded on your merits per subject rather than having to excel at them all.

I left school at fourteen and went straight to work in a local bakery called Kennedy's. It was my first real job and I thoroughly enjoyed it as it gave me an invaluable experience of working life, although I never intended it to fulfil my life's dreams! The money was good, but the tasks involved became very mundane and I found myself getting bored after a time. Eventually I decided to give myself more of a challenge and took a job in a weaving mill in Harolds Cross. It was housed in a very old building that was poorly lit and quite eerie at night. Shadows could play tricks on your eyes but on several occasions I knew that what I had seen there was more than just a trick of the light. From time to time I would see an old lady gliding gracefully across the mill room floors as if on her way to an appointment or meeting. No one else though had ever seen her. In my time at the mill I learned to make all sorts of things; patterns, coats, coverings, and so on. I had a very good time there and made lots of friends. There was always a lot of variety involved in the jobs that we could do, and so I never minded working overtime, indeed it is nice to get paid extra doing something that you enjoy. One particular summers evening, several of us were working over and one of the girls, Angela commented that she would really love a big juicy apple. I jokingly replied "There's some at the back of the mill but you'll have a hard time reaching them". There was a large wall at the back of the mill fencing it off from the neighbouring residential area. One of the homes on the other side of the wall had a large orchard whose branches overhung the wall slightly. We all knew this tree was plentiful with apples and so another friend, Caroline replied "I know where there's a ladder" and proceeded to it's location. In the back of my mind I could hear my grandmother saying "You'll all be ill in the morning because they are cooking apples and not yet ripe." My grandmother I have always considered to be my conscience and whenever I am about to do something I shouldn't I wait for her voice to pipe up. On this instance however, despite me relaying the warning to my friends, we proceeded with our plan. Angela was already upon the wall throwing down apples to us and looking cautiously to see if we were being watched. We had more apples than we could eat that night. As we were putting the ladder away Angela piped up "See I told you no one was looking". It didn't put my mind at rest though as my grandmother was always right. Nothing was to happen that night.

The next morning, however, was a different matter. Not only were we feeling off colour but were cornered by the gentleman who owned the house. He told us that the next time we wanted to pinch his apples not to bother as we would only have to knock on his door and he would give us some. He told us that he had been watching us from the bedroom window. He then put a brown paper bag down on the desk and said "How are you all feeling today ladies?" Of course he knew how we felt; our red faces giving all away. "You can have these apples as well and they should make you feel a lot better". We were to learn that this man was a floor manager in another part of the factory. Once again my grandmother had smacked my hand from the spirit world and would do so again on many future occasions.

I had tried to keep in contact with my friends on The Coombe but sadly it became impossible as our new flat was a fair distance away from what was left of our old home. Josie, in particular, was a friend I missed but since she had moved too, and in the opposite direction to us, our meetings were very rare. The only real contact I had with Josie was through her father, Thomas, who worked nearby. We would often stop to chat about what was happening in our families' lives. One day I arrived home from work. I was by now about sixteen years old. My mother stopped me at the door and told me that, very sadly, Thomas had died and I should go over to the family and pass on her condolences for their great loss. If Josie needed me to spend the night, I was to do so as the proceeding day was a Saturday so I didn't have to go to work. I went to Josies that night and tried to offer some comfort to her and her family who were naturally all devastated. Thomas had been a fit and healthy man but had been taken from this world by a heart attack. It was a sad time for Josie and her family, she was now married and had a young baby and was indeed wed to a brute for a husband as I had predicted earlier and sleeping on her mothers floor as well. So as you can imagine, poor Josie had suffered another terrible blow at a very sensitive time. I decided that I would spend the night with her and later in the evening we retired. We lay awake for some time chatting and reminiscing about Thomas. Josie said that she would love to hear her father locking and bolting the door and switching off the lights as he used to do every night. "Oh but you will" I replied. Thinking no more of it, our conversation turned to the time when her father had caught us both smoking a whole pack of Woodbines. We were literally blue in the face and sitting in a room resembling an opium den but Thomas just smiled at us and never said a word; a lucky escape! We both giggled. Just then we both heard a sound downstairs that made us jump; the front door was being bolted and we could here footsteps up the stairs. We both knew it was Thomas. I quickly said "God bless you Tommy". It was wonderful to know that even now he was making sure we were safe and secure for the night because our loved ones often come to look over us, especially when we are most vulnerable. We both felt very safe and happy that night. Over the years I have often noticed Thomas coming back to say "Hello" and I wish him well on his spiritual journey.

****

I remained a worker at the mill for some time after this. It was a job I enjoyed and the money I was making not only helped to support the family but gave me the chance to save up for my first holiday - to England. It was the end of July and I only had a few more days to wait before this great adventure, which was something I had wanted to do all my life. I was going with some friends on the ferry, or cattle boat, as we then called it. We had planned to go to Cheshire and stay with my friends family and it was going to be wonderful. Then I started to get the pain. It was on my right hand side near my stomach and I knew in my heart that it was appendicitis. I was aware that if I brought it to a doctors attention I would be merrily whisked away to hospital and my holiday would be cancelled. Well, not as far as I was concerned, so I kept my mouth shut. On the Sunday night before we were due to go, my friend Pauline and I were standing in the hallway of the flat. We were about to say "Goodnight" to each other when she gave me a strange look. I asked her "Why are you looking at me like that?" and she replied "Your face is glowing in the dark. It's all green and glowing. Are you feeling all right?". I snapped back "I'm fine. It's just your imagination" She repeated it again and then said her farewells. She was, however, correct; I was in a lot of pain, so much so that I didn't sleep very well that night.

I went to work as usual for the next three days. On the Wednesday morning I was very excited as I was sailing to England that night. I still felt terrible but no one knew of my secret so I would make it to the boat. I was supposed to meet Clare for lunch that day as she too was working at the mill with me but when I went to look for her she was nowhere to be found as the manager had let her go a little earlier than usual. I thought that this was a very peculiar action as he was not normally the type of person to do something like that. I proceeded to walk home on my own and was met by my mother at the door, looking very stern. "I have run a bath for you young lady and when you've had it the only place you'll be going to is to the hospital" she stated. How on earth did my mother know I was ill since I had been so careful not to let it show?

At the hospital I was examined and put in a wheelchair as I had a very high temperature. The doctor was adamant that I would not be walking up to the ward as my temperature was rocketing. He was admitting me immediately. I felt angry and heartbroken that my dream holiday had been taken away from me when I had tried so hard to control the situation. I was put to bed and given an injection to try and bring my temperature down as they could not operate until my body was behaving more normally.

That night my sister and her friend Lily, whom I knew very well, arrived before the rest of my family. We began joking about my holiday, although it was still not very amusing to me. Lily quipped, "The only boat you'll be sailing in tonight is your bed!" I looked at her and pointed at a bed at the other side of the ward and jokingly replied that that bed would stay empty until the weekend as it was especially for her. She giggled and retorted "The only place I'll be this weekend is at my sister's wedding. I'm the chief bridesmaid!" "Oh you will be at the wedding", I replied, "but in the afternoon you'll still be in that bed, flat on your back, just as I will be". I then asked my sister how mother had known I was ill when I had not told anyone. Apparently our manager had sent her home to tell mum that if she did not get her daughter to the hospital straight away and stop her going to England then she would be coming home to her in a box as I had got DEATH written all over my face. He had told her to make sure to tell my mother that he had the gift of second sight, and she would understand what he meant. As I have already said, I have many guardian angels, not only in spirit but on this earth as well.

I was like a pin cushion from the constant injections over the next few days, as my temperature would not go down. I hadn't eaten anything for nearly three days as the medical staff were on standby to operate as soon as they could. My appendix was getting very bad and everyone was afraid that it was going to rupture so an operation would need to be conducted, fever or not. On Saturday morning my temperature finally went down and I was taken to theatre where my appendix was removed. The next thing I remember was a lady in the next bed on the ward calling to me, saying that my friend Lily was here. I looked up expecting to see her but was told that she was over in the bed that had stood empty all week. I could not believe what I was hearing! It appears that Lily had been eating gooseberries at the wedding reception and thought that they were giving her tummy pains. The pain had got so bad that she had been rushed to hospital and was diagnosed as having a ruptured appendix! What I'd said in jest had turned out to be true. What I was in fact doing was relaying a message from the spirit world, but I had not realised this at the time.

It was enough to put me off utilising my gift for a long time. Everyone but myself could see the funny side of it. My mouth was too blunt and my gift unchanneled and I didn't want it anymore. I felt as if I had wished my sisters friend into that bed and I was angry. As you know, it wasn't the first time that I had said something in jest that had transpired into reality. I now know that all this was because my gift was flowing so freely and I had not learned how to control it or even realise when I was using it.

Lily and I became close friends after this incident and I now appreciate that I had been sent a friend to keep me company during my recovery. I also thank my grandmother for her watchful eye and my manager from the mill for his intervention which had saved my life and what would have been a premature passing.

I believe that everything happens for a reason and I understand that these things had a lot to teach me about the forces within this universe and the gift that I possess. These events which I detail to you were constructed so that I could pass them on to you, through this book and in my work to bring enlightenment and comfort. It was many years before I revealed my gift to the world. It was a great burden at times to hold back something so special but I now know that I should never have feared it because it was given to me to help others and that is what I must do. Everyone has a role to play in this life, be it great or small, but sometimes the smallest role can turn into the greatest one of all. I know using my gift for the benefit of others is mine. We are all a link in a chain which will continue to grow long after you and I have left this plain and this link extends beyond into the spirit world because, after all, life is everlasting.

4

Joe

I remember having a dream in which I was talking to my grandmother. We were having a conversation about the man I was going to marry. She told me she was sent to show him to me in a dream and to watch carefully as I should remember everything that I was about to be shown. I got up and walked over and stood beside her. She lifted her hand out in front of her and brought it round from her left side to right. As she did this the space in front of us rippled and fell away, being replaced by something entirely different and exciting. There was lots of noise from crowds of people and lights flashing everywhere. I could see people at a fairground ride, the one with chairs that spin up in the air, laughing and shouting and obviously having a wonderful time. Fifties music was everywhere. Then the lights went out on it. "Watch closely, for here is the man you will marry", whispered my grandmother in my ear. As I watched, a young man walked in front of us towards the ride "I'll have this fixed in a few minutes" I heard him say. He began adjusting the wiring of the lights and sure enough, he got them working again. He turned to the crowd of people and took a bow as a huge cheer went up and the ride resumed. I looked closer at him. He had a fifties hairstyle, like Elvis Presley and his face was very kind. I could feel he had a tremendous sense of humour. I remember thinking to myself, is he going to work in a fair and will we be travelling all over the place? My grandmother, sensing my thoughts answered "You will meet him soon and know the answers to your questions then." I wish I could have spoken to him. The next thing I remember is grandmother waving her arm again and me waking up in bed.

Three weeks later I met Joe at a discotheque. I was out with my friend Mary and we were having a wonderful time. It was July 1965 and so many good records were around then; The Beatles, Rolling Stones and the Motown sound were all in full flow. It was a good time to be young. At some point in the evening, Joe came up to talk to Mary and we said "Hello" and not much else. Shortly after, I was dancing when Mary came up to me and said that Joe had been watching me all night!

At the end of the night we began our walk home. It was a considerable distance away but we enjoyed it. I suppose we had little choice about it though! After a while a car pulled up beside us. There were several young men in it and they asked us if we knew the way to one of the dance halls out of town. We gave them directions and were just about to resume our journey when they asked if we wanted to join them. "No thank you" I replied, unprepared to get into a car of strange men. "Don't be a spoilsport" said Mary but I stuck to my guns and we continued to walk home. We walked in silence for a while, Mary was probably angry that her night out had been cut short but I cannot be sure. From behind us we heard music so we stopped and turned. There was a man I'd never seen before and Joe! He was carrying a small radio. We waited for them to catch up and continued to walk together. As we walked and talked I was amazed at how much we had in common. We both loved music and going to the cinema and Joe had spent some time studying drama at the Abbey Theatre. I found this fascinating. My experience of my grandmother showing Joe to me in a dream was becoming more clear with each step. I had actually met Joe before about two years ago, and had seen him around since, in fact, I was able to describe to him exactly what he was wearing and how he wore his hair. He was enchanting and we decided to meet up again.

Over the next few days, I spent a lot of time with Joe and began to learn more about both him and his family. I learned that he was one of eight children and was shown the family home which was located near Crumlin in Dublin. He spent time there but also worked and lived over in England, in both Huddersfield and Leeds. His mother had left the family when he was fourteen and no one knew where she'd gone. I was sad for him when I heard this because my father had never been around very much when I was growing up. Joe doubted that he would ever see her again. I knew better and I went on to describe something to him that I had seen in a dream the night before. There had been a woman looking from a window. She had black hair and wore glasses. She was wearing a wraparound apron. Joe got up from his chair and went to the drawer he took out a photo of his mother and showed it to me. It was the woman I had seen in my dreams. I then went on to tell him that they would be united again one day, which he seemed to doubt, but it did come to pass in 1982.

****

A short while after I was struck ill again. It was about a week after I had met Joe and found that I was developing a sore throat. I felt very poorly when I got to work so I left after ten minutes and went home to bed with a hot toddy where I drifted into an uneasy sleep. The next day I was much worse, but I continued to underplay it to my family. Over the following hours I found myself drifting in and out of consciousness. My mother was very worried and insisted she cancel a meeting with a friend to sit with me but I demanded she went and not be so silly. In retrospect now I should not have let her go, but I am a strong minded person and do not like a fuss to be made of me unnecessarily. I tried to sleep, but it was impossible. Someone knocked at our door for about ten minutes and then started calling me through the letter box. I sluggishly dragged myself from the warm refuge of my bed to answer the door. A friend of mine stood there. I tried to explain to her that I was ill and just wanted to lie down, but she kept me talking for what seemed like an eternity. I couldn't even break away to put a dressing gown and slippers on. Eventually, she departed and left me to struggle back to my bed alone.

At some point during the next day I knew I was near the point of death. I was lying in bed not knowing what was happening to me. I saw myself drifting down a long dark tunnel. Everything was still and peaceful. I was in awe at the tranquillity and calm I was feeling. In the distance I could see shapes moving towards me, emerging from a still distant light. As they approached me, I realised that one was my grandmother and the other a stranger, bathed in white light. My grandfather was gliding gracefully behind. I heard my grandmother's voice, yet I was aware that she was not using her mouth as she was in front of me, her face transfixed with a smile. I heard her say "You must go back now. Open your eyes and tell your mother to get you a doctor straight away." I did as she requested and opened my eyes to find myself back in bed with my mother's ear pressed against my face.

She gasped with relief when she saw I was conscious and said "I'm getting you a doctor now". I expressed my agreement with her as she hurriedly left the room.
She returned shortly after, explaining to the doctor how she had walked in to see me lying motionless on the bed, my face ashen coloured and not breathing. She had been checking to see if I was still alive. The doctor proceeded to my bedside and examined me. He determined that I had the misfortune of developing both pneumonia and tonsillitis at the same time. I was extremely weak and he was reluctant to move me for fear of killing me but informed us that he would have a bed on standby at the hospital if I needed it. He remained with me for the next few hours and made sure that I responded to the medication he had administered and then left. I knew it was not my time to go and I would be all right now. Slowly over the next few days I began to grow stronger again and recover. My near death experience still remains one of my most vivid and spectacular memories and I know that the moment of death, where we complete our transposition from this life to the next, is not something to fear but should be celebrated, as we are following a pathway to a life where everything is beautiful and family and friends await us.
When I was fully recovered, I continued to see Joe and just before Christmas in 1965, he proposed. I accepted, of course and we planned to marry at Christmas in 1966. In the February month of that year we began tentative preparations, which began with the selection of an engagement ring. We went to the jewellers and saw the ring I wanted, my nose pressed up against the window, it was the most beautiful ring we had seen and it was at the right price too. We could not actually buy the ring at that time, instead we were to return for it in March as our official engagement would take place

on my birthday. I closed my eyes and prayed to God that my ring would still be there then.

That evening, it was a Friday, I was waiting for Joe to call for me, and we were going to go to the cinema, as was now customary with us at this point of the week. At this same time, a relative of ours was staying with us, called Pat. He was in the living room this particular evening, playing with a pack of cards. When I saw this I asked him what he could see in them for me. My mother stopped and asked "Can you see?"

"Yes", replied Pat and began spreading out the cards on the table to answer my question. He began, "You will have a ring on your finger very soon and will marry somewhere other than the church you have chosen. You will also be married much sooner than you think". He also told me I should take better care of my health.

Later that evening, Joe arrived and I told him of how Pat had read my cards. This upset Joe a little but it took time to find out why. We walked for a little while and suddenly he stopped and turned, saying "I have something to tell you. I'm sorry Pat told you about the ring as I was going to surprise you. I was going to take you into town tomorrow for your engagement ring". So the first part of Pat's prediction was already coming true. In fact all of what Pat had said did come to pass. We had initially planned to be married at St. Teresas Church on Boxing Day but that did not transpire. Instead we were wed at St. Marys in Crewe, Cheshire on the first of October. Quite a strange turn of events but this is an example of how I have followed a very set path in my life and my move to England was one of its many turns.

I had always told my friends that I would live in England one day. I never knew why or how, I just knew. It was in early August that the bombshell dropped. Joe was made redundant and there was little chance of another job being found in Ireland as things were desperate. My brother was living in Cheshire, England with his new family and fate just seemed to indicate that we should join them, so we made our way to England on the ferry to Liverpool and via train to Crewe. I was thinking to myself, well you're finally here girl. This is what you have been talking about for as long as you can recall.

We arrived in Crewe and were very lucky to get jobs straight away so we decided to set the date for our wedding, October 1st. We had already bought our wedding outfits and brought them over with us and preparations were going well until the week we were to be married. Joe was told he would be made redundant on the Friday, the day before our wedding. It was a terrible blow. We had very little money and already we were having problems. We were three pounds ten shillings short for the flower arrangements and Joe was getting irate because we knew not where the money would come from. I kept telling him it would be okay and the money would come from somewhere. Sure enough, it did. The very next day as we got in from work there was a letter waiting for us. When we opened it out popped three pounds and a ten shilling note - exactly the amount we needed. It was a present from family in Ireland. I could feel the relief that went through Joe.

On the Friday night before our big day, Joe's friends began arriving from Leeds, as Joe knew a lot of people from working up there in the past. Among them was his best man. They stayed with my brothers' in-laws on the next street. The wedding went beautifully and was a wonderful day, not bad, considering it was three months early! We went home after the ceremony and quickly got changed before we set off for our honeymoon - in Liverpool! We went to the famous

Beatles Cavern and walked along the docks. I couldn't have been happier.
Upon our return to Crewe, we made a snap decision to move up to Leeds as there was a promise of work up there and Joe had contacts who could help us set up home. So off we went again on the train to another magical city.
When we got to Leeds, we immediately approached Joe's old landlady for a room. It was unfortunate but she did not have any rooms to let but was kind enough to let us sleep on her living room floor for our first night there. The next morning, we secured our very own flat, and our first home together. New jobs followed shortly after. It was all falling into place now. I was used to living in flats, and this as was now a tradition for me, was on the top floor. It was on Avenue Hill and overlooked Potter Newton Park. There were wonderful carnivals here in the summer, which we could watch from the comfort of our own home! We stayed in the flat for over two years and had many happy memories there.
I went to work in a weaving mill called Dixons, which was just off Kirkstall Road. Sadly, it is not there anymore and I often wonder where all the girls are that I once worked with as we got on so well together. I had three friends in particular, Lynn, Jean and Marie. We would often meet for lunch in the cloakroom. It was not practical to go anywhere else as we only had half an hour. One day when I was a little late in joining them, I walked in to find them all huddled over a Ouija board. I couldn't believe my eyes. Immediately, I asked them to stop using it, as it would only tell them lies and no good would come of it. They asked me if I could move it, to which I replied I could but I would not use it. They were having difficulty getting it to move at all and kept asking me to try. As I walked closer I saw a man in the corner of the room, he was in spirit so I alone could see him. He

was motioning for me to touch the board. I said out loud that I would move the pointer but no more and asked God for protection in my mind. Outwards went my hand to touch the pointer. As we connected, it moved and proceeded to dart across the board frantically. The girls looked on in amazement, for they did not know of my gift as I no longer spoke of or used it. I could sense their curiosity but before they could ask me any questions I withdrew my hand and left the room, quite annoyed by the whole thing. I must stress to you at this point that you must NEVER use a Ouija board. You are opening up yourself to forces that you will have little or no control over and putting yourself into a great deal of danger. They are not toys but a peripheral to the spiritual plain used by those spirits who revel in malevolent and wicked intention. Stay away from them.

My experience that day awakened me to my gift again and I should have known that it would only be a matter of time before the spirit world made another bid to convince me I should be using my gift. I was having dinner with Joe. It seemed to me like a perfectly normal evening, until Joe got up and announced he had a surprise for me and I should go and put my coat on as we were going out for a while. I kept probing for more information but none was forthcoming so I resigned myself to the fact that I would know about it when we got there. Joe actually took me to my first Spiritual meeting on that evening.

I don't know what made him take me that particular night. It may have been because he wanted me to see the speaker on the rostrum that night, who was called Fred Moor. I found myself immensely drawn into what he was saying to the congregation and was amazed at how freely the gift of clairvoyance flowed from him. I never dreamed that he would approach me with a message, but do just that he did.

He told me that my grandmother was stood behind me and she was saying to tell me that there was Scots blood in the family and to stop worrying all the time about my mother as she would be around for a good few years yet! He then went on to say that I would return to this place and pointed at the rostrum on which he stood, "You know what she means" he laughed, "she has always watched over you and always will" he concluded. At the end of the service we chatted briefly and shook hands. "You will be back".

As we made our way home I reflected on the events of the evening. At that point I had absolutely no intention of returning there. I had shut my gift off and did not intend to use it again. How wrong I was! It was fated that I attend that service because it truly was a turning point in my spiritual life, a reminder that I had been bestowed with something very special. We all know how the spirit world can sometimes work in mysterious ways.

5

Life In The Seventies

As time marched on, we were able to amass a small deposit for our first home. We had been renting our flat for some time now and I couldn't help but feel that the time was right for us to find a place of our own. There is something very different in the feel of a property that you own as oppose to rent. It just seems more homely. We'd seen a little back to back advertised in the local paper and decided to chase it up. The property was situated quite close to the flat we were renting, just off Roundhay Road, and so one evening we decided to take a walk down there and have a look at it. When we came to the house we found it was vacant so we couldn't actually look inside but it looked decent enough from the outside. After peering through the windows we found it to be in like condition inside. I knew that this would be our new home. On the way home we discussed how we would call the estate agent in the morning. The next day Joe rang to arrange a viewing appointment but was told by the agent that the house had been sold. I knew this was not so and I got a bus into town on my lunch hour to find out what was happening. When I reached their office I was told that in fact the house had not been sold, it was simply a misunderstanding as the keys hadn't been returned, but if I would come back the following day they would be there for me to collect. Everything from then on in went smoothly and we moved into the house within the month. The estate agent was even kind enough to lend us the keys in the interim to allow us to decorate. I know that it was my grandmother's influence that made me go down to the estate agents that day as she knew that the house was meant to be ours. As it worked out, less than two weeks before we moved our landlady came and told us we would have to be out of the flat as she needed the space for her own family, so I do believe that the spirit world were hard at work behind the scenes knowing that this was about to happen.

Over the next couple of years we worked on our home and turned it into a palace. Everything we made went on the house to make it as special as possible. We had to buy furniture from scratch as our flat had been furnished and a new kitchen and bathroom had to be put in as our bath had been in the kitchen! The electrics were re-wired by Joe (harking back to my vision, when Joe repaired the electrics of the fairground ride) and we then finally had hot water, as the house had no means of heating it before this other than a kettle or pan. Things were going well, perhaps a little too well, and as is customary when you start to get complacent, something comes along to snap you back on your feet again. Joe was made redundant from the warehouse he had worked in for three years as it was closing down. This meant we had to do some serious re-evaluation and Joe decided that he would become a self-employed disc jockey. There was no danger in being made redundant if he did that, he had been made redundant in Dublin, Crewe and now Leeds! We went around looking at turntables and speakers and quite soon he had everything he needed to do the job. He had already amassed a considerable record collection and had the musical knowledge and talent to do very well. When he started, he quickly built up a reputation and packed many venues out. Soon he was known across Leeds as "Disco Joe"! I have very happy memories of those times.

We were once again very comfortable and secure which was probably just as well as about a year after Joe started playing records I found I was pregnant. I always thought I had a hearty appetite but I scaled to new heights during my pregnancy. It used to drive Joe to despair as I would constantly be sending him out for large quantities of my favourite foods, especially fish cakes. But, not just any fish cake, they had to be from a shop in Armley, on the other side of Leeds!

I had a good pregnancy up until the last six weeks, when for some reason my blood pressure shot up dramatically. I was told by the hospital to stay in bed for the next week which I did, after all, what heavily pregnant woman wouldn't like to be pampered for a week! Unfortunately though, this did not seem to help me and so they admitted me to St. James Hospital shortly after. Two days later, when the doctor found my blood pressure had not gone down, he decided to induce the birth immediately.

As the contractions got stronger I was moved into the labour ward on the Friday evening. I was dozing and mumbling out loud at the same time. I had a vision that I remember quite vividly. I saw Joe in a betting shop tearing up a piece of paper. Minnie Cauldwell and Ena Sharples were talking to him, so it was obviously a set from Coronation Street. Just then I opened my eyes and saw Joe and his sister Eileen standing over me. I told him what I had seen and everyone had a good laugh about it. Joe had studied drama in Ireland and had had a part in the film "The Girl With The Green Eyes". He had just signed with an agent in Leeds for some 'extra' work, as acting was something that Joe had a passion for. So in hindsight my vision did not seem out of place. I was to be in labour for the next two days and concern was growing for both mine and the baby's welfare. It was about 4:45 pm when the doctor walked in to the delivery room with a pair of forceps. This sent me into a mental spasm as I did not want our baby born with the help of forceps. I was told that if nothing happened within the next twenty minutes they would have to use them. As they left the room I prayed out loud to God to let me bring this baby into the world by myself, as Mary had given birth to Jesus in a stable. When I finished my prayer, things started to happen! Our son was born at 4:48 pm weighing 7 lb and 15 oz. He was active from the first moment and didn't even wait to wet his nappy, preferring a nurses arm instead! As I held him in my arms for the first time I kissed him once for health and once for happiness and was so very grateful and relieved that he had come into the world unaided. We named our son Alan, after the 1940's movie star Alan Ladd as we had been very moved by his performance in the classic western "Shane". Alan had arrived in this world eleven days earlier than expected. I was hoping that everything would go smoothly from this point but somewhere in the back of my mind there was a nagging doubt that there was more to come. Both Alan and I had problems due to the length and intensity of labour. He was in intensive care for two days after the birth and I had complications. My stay in hospital was supposed to have been forty-eight hours, instead this turned into ten days. I thought I was never going to get out of Jimmys! Alan is an only child, I did miscarry a little girl and have been told that I miscarried another boy as well who are now both growing happily in spirit.

Mother and Child

As you laid me down to rest
You kissed me gently
Your sweet breath upon my face
As you held me in your warm embrace

You did not want to let me go
You fought for me through thick and thin
But you always knew that death would win
A smile was always on your face

You stood firm in faith and grace
All the heartache there within
Hidden deep the sob behind your troth
You never gave up hope

You wiped away my every tear
You took away my very fear
My days grew short my body frail
And still the strength in you prevailed

My last hour came you held me close
You spoke about the promised land
And told me all about God's plan
The things of beauty I'd see there

In strength and beauty I would grow
Free from pain and all the tears
That I had suffered in my wee small years
And God would take me in his hand

And show to me his wondrous plan
Suddenly I felt so light
As I moved forwards t'ward the light
Now I wear a gown so white

About my head are daises bright
And now I walk within your dreams
Talk to you of things I've seen
As you sit and count the days

Your mind still whirling and in a daze
I will be there at every turn
And walk beside you 'till your journeys done
You and I will dance with glee
As reunited we will be

Alan is grown up now and stands at 6' 4", and has his own semi-detached house! He is very literate and writes music and is currently trying for his own career on the stage. As for the scene I foresaw of Joe playing in Coronation Street, he got a call a couple of weeks later and told to report to Granada for filming of the show as an extra. He has appeared on the show many times now and was fondly known by many of the cast. I myself have been on the set and watched them work and found it to be a mesmerising experience.
We stayed in our little home for a time after Alan was born but just before his second birthday, we decided we should move house as we were living very close to two major roads and there was no garden for Alan to play in. We sat down and did our homework and decided that we just might be able to get a good deposit for a semi-detached if we could get the right price for our back to back and as we'd done a lot of work on it, we did not think that this was unreasonable. We had looked at a few but we either did not like them or they were too expensive. We were about to resign ourselves to the fact that it was not going to happen when we came across the perfect house, quite by accident,

as we returned home one day. We got out of our van to have a look at it and found for the second time that this house too was vacant. Joe took to it straight away, but I felt less optimistic. As we got back in the van we noticed the sale board was for the same agents we had dealt with when we had bought our first home. We decided to call the agent when we got home and agreed that we could pay up to £6,900 for the house. As soon as we walked through the door I phoned them up and explained the situation. As I spoke to the agent, he informed me that the house was £6,900 and it was not subject to any offers! You can imagine my reaction. I found it very odd at the time and realised that this house must surely be our next home. We got the keys the next day to have a look around it. The house was generally in good condition but was in need of modernisation and decoration. This in itself was not so bad as we were experts at home decoration by now. There was something in the back of my mind though that did not sit right, some niggling feeling that this was all coming too easy. I just couldn't shake this feeling off, yet I didn't quite know what was causing all this to bother me. Whatever I thought, Joe did like this house. It was a quiet tranquil area, close to the local amenities, and had lots of garden for Alan to explore so we decided to buy. Our old home was sold immediately. It all happened so fast in fact, that my unease about the situation did not have time to settle until it was too late. The contracts were signed and the house was ours.

The house over the course of the next seven years was to be the setting for a myriad of heartache and despair. Upon moving in, immediately revealed to me was a loathsome and miserable presence which existed deep into the very foundations. So much had happened in the house before we had moved in as I was soon to discover. The previous owners, an elderly woman and her spinster daughter had met with tragedy. The old lady had outlived her daughter who had died of a heart attack just outside the house in the middle of the road. The old woman, who was unable to care for herself, had been put into a home, hence we were able to aquire the house so cheaply as there was a considerable need to sell. The next-door neighbour once told me how the daughter would continually come round in the early hours of the morning and complain to her about the banging on the wall, which my neighbour assured me was not their doing as they were all in bed and asleep in her household. I should have realised this was a sign of impending doom for us.

As we settled in I noticed that Alan didn't like staying on his own upstairs during the day and never used his bedroom. This was even more the case at night and would create havoc if we did not leave the light on for him. Alan, like myself, is a natural gifted medium from birth and has seen spirit from as far back as I can remember, but this house is the only house I can say he was frightened of living in. As for me I always face my fears head on, but this house had a way of getting to me through my own family. It knew that it could not disturb me through my own anxieties so played on those of my loved ones. If it had not been for the protection of my grandmother and others in spirit I dare not contemplate what other possible misery may have been wrought by this house. It did everything in its power to destroy my family and I longed for the day when we would be able to leave it far behind.

Alan, as he was growing up, in his own little way was becoming more and more aware of the things that were happening. Many a night I would leave the downstairs light on for him in case he wondered downstairs in the small hours. Usually though, the light would stay on for about five minutes before someone or something would switch it off. Alan would stay as close to me as he could during the evening and would not be left alone in any room that was not well lit. Alan was always able to pick up good, or bad, vibrations from a young age, just as I had been able to do in my childhood. Therefore I was able to reach out to him and make him feel secure. It was also to be of help to him when he began to see the spirit people who would pass through our house.

On one occasion my mother was visiting from Crewe and suggested I had a night out with some friends at the venue Joe was playing and she would baby-sit. She no doubt expected that the evening would be a rare but peaceful time spent between herself and Alan - she was wrong! It was quite late that evening when we got home. My mother always liked to stay up until everyone was safely home. As it happened Alan was still awake as mother had brought him down because he'd refused to settle. She was holding him in her arms as we walked in. As Joe took him from my mothers' arms Alan pointed to a corner by the window and asked "Daddy, who is that man standing in the corner?" Joe replied "Which man? What does he look like?" Alan replied, "He's a big man with a coat and a hat on". By this time my mother was in a terrible state and asked me to fetch some holy water and bless that corner of the room as she wouldn't sleep a wink that night if I didn't. In the meantime it was a thousand-and-one questions from Joe who was finding it most fascinating and Alan, for once, did not seem in the least perturbed by the experience. As I sprinkled the holy water in the corner Alan asked "Daddy, why is mummy throwing water over the man, 'cause he's going now". I knew that there was nothing to be afraid of that night as the figure had actually been my mother's brother, John, who had simply been there that night to watch over my family.

To us, Alan never was a baby. He seemed to grow up so quickly both mentally and spiritually. He had very developed speech around the time of this incident (he was about three years old) and would often talk to us of times when he was a man like his daddy. He seemed to have very vivid recollection of previous lives. I only wish in hindsight that we could have taken more time to talk to him about these memories and explore them more, perhaps even recorded them on tape. There are many similar children around the world who can relate similar experiences, so if one of them is yours, do please talk about it. It is a unique experience you may never have again.

There was another, very emotional instance, where Alan has seen spirit in the house. Joe was resident D.J. at a very popular venue just off York Road. It was a place owned by a lovely couple, Jenny and Jim. They were a pleasure to work for and became good friends. Some time after we first became acquainted, Jenny's mother died. It was a terrible blow to her and it was something she never really came to terms with. This, and an accumulation of other events, took it's toll on poor Jenny and she took her own life. It was devastating to me, especially as she'd confided in me on several occasions that she had thought about doing it. I had done my utmost to persuade her that it was wrong and that no matter how bad things seem one must not give up hope as they will always get better, but it was no good.

We attended Jenny's funeral, and decided to leave Alan at home as it would no doubt prove to be quite a traumatic experience for him. It was a beautiful service. When we returned home, we found that Alan had been the receptacle of quite an unusual experience. He told us how he had been watching television and had got up to go to the kitchen to get a drink of juice. He described to us how he felt an urge to turn back and look into the living room as he reached the door. There in the chair nearest the window he saw Jenny, dressed in a blue outfit and bathed in a soft, glowing light. She had smiled at him and motioned for him to come over and sit on her knee, with which he had complied. He confessed to finding it quite strange that when he had sat with her she had disappeared. Jenny had always been extremely fond of Alan and I truly believe that this was her way of making sure he was okay whilst we were out and of saying goodbye to him. God bless you Jenny. We miss you.

The pub that Jenny owned was a great place, although after her death it seemed to lose a sigificant amount of its feeling. Nevertheless, Joe continued to work there and pack them in. I often went with him on the nights he played there, partly because I liked to keep my eye on how Jenny's family were coping and also because one of my closest friends was working there. Her name was Sara.

Sara was a member of the bar staff. She was, and still is, one of the most delightful people I have ever met. We had hit it off instantly as we were very much on a similar wavelength. Sara and I could talk for hours and knew each other very well. At the point after Jenny's death, we were all feeling a little down and depressed and Sara was no exception. I remember talking to her one night about her settling down and having children. Sara wasn't seeing anyone special at the time and was explaining to me how unlikely it was that she would have children as she had a medical problem that would cause complications. Me, being my usual self perked up "Of course you'll have a child!" Sara disagreed and I reprimanded and so it went on for about two minutes when I finally broke the circle and said "You will have at least one child; a boy, but you won't accept that you are pregnant at the time". Sara looked at me, puzzled and asked how I should know such a thing. "Just a hunch" I replied, "or you could call it a sixth sense if you like". As I have said, I never revealed the true source of my gift to anyone, not even Sara. As time went on, Sara did indeed meet a man whom she went on to marry, and, when she least expected it, found herself pregnant. She gave birth to a wonderful, healthy baby boy who has grown up to be a fine young man. So those in the spirit world were right, and I'm very happy that I had a part to play in Sara's life. There is still a spiritual bond between us even though we do not see each other very often. We still send cards for birthdays and Christmas. Thank you Sara for being a wonderful, caring person who kept me going when everything seemed to be going wrong in my life.

As Alan grew up, we were hoping he would deal with his fears of the house but even as he approached six years of age, he still wouldn't go upstairs without one of us. He was still sleeping with the light on and continually waking up through the night. The atmosphere in the house was growing darker - it was as if misery and depression were bleeding from the walls and the terrible energies were beginning to take their toll on Joe. I was very aware of what was going on here, but was powerless to do anything about it. The entity concerned, a woman, was very clever indeed. She would send forth her negativity but would stay just far enough in the shadows to stop me from reaching to her. She was a lost soul, who had no desire to be rescued and lead onwards. She was quite content to remain with us and revel in her sadistic pleasures. I tried to pray for her and help her so that she would find peace, but she was too resistant and too much a part of the house to move on. I do not believe that this being was the daughter who had died so young, rather a lost soul who had gone wondering and become attached to the house. This would classify her as a classic haunting. Hauntings involve spirits who remain within a certain area. It is usually a place where there is tremendous psychic energy which draws them like magnets. They are often entities that do not even realise that they have passed on and vent their frustration at the intrusion on "their" property in very negative ways. The property may even at one time have belonged to them hence they feel their actions are justified and any steps they take to protect their homes are warranted. Sometimes though, it can be an angry spirit that takes ownership of the place. They are usually drawn to areas that exhibit strong negative vibrations. These entities are often aware that they have left us and are in existence somewhere else, yet they like to abuse the power relations between our dimensions and wreak havoc on the Earth plain. Not all places that are haunted are necessarily bad. Sometimes it is the actions of ourselves that cause the problem, such as using a Ouija board. Whatever the cause, I was never quite sure what had brought our tormentor to our house.

I watched Joe become more and more unsettled as time went on, and saw a good man turn into a wreck. He began to do things that were so out of character. He became snappy and irritable all the time. He was surviving on just two or three hours of sleep a night. He hardly ate any more and despite all my efforts I could not persuade him to see what he was doing to himself and confront it. I was at my wits end. The weaker he got, the stronger she got. In the end I forced Joe to go see a doctor, but the rot had set in. His weight had plummeted to around nine stone and his six foot frame was skeletal. There came a point when he came to say that he couldn't care less if he lived or died. I was looking at a zombie by this time. He began walking the streets all day

and would not return home until it was time to get ready for work in the evening. Even then he still refused to eat.
One day he arrived home and I again tried to coax him into eating but this time it only seemed to make matters worse. On that particular day, to ease the situation I took Alan down to Roundhay Road for a walk and to do a little shopping at the same time. When we had finished, we stopped at a friends house who lived on our route home. Her name was Charmaine. She had the kettle on when we got there and offered Alan a fruit juice. Just as she started to pour the juice I jumped up, and stated that we had to go as I needed to get home, saying that I had not realised the time. I suddenly felt an immense pressure to get home as soon as possible. I knew I was needed there right away. As I walked in the door, I was told to go upstairs as I knew Joe was up there. When I reached our room and opened the door, I found him lying on the bed. He had been taking anti-depressants for his persistent mood swings and, giving in to the malevolent force around us, had taken the entire bottle at once. He was barely conscious at the time I found him. I quickly ran downstairs and called an ambulance. I then went back upstairs and tried to wake Joe up, which was practically impossible. I kept talking to him and shaking him, forcing him to stay with me at least in part, until the ambulance could get here.
When it finally arrived, we were taken to St. James's Hospital where Joe had his stomach pumped. The effect of the tablets though were well and truly in his system and he was quite delirious. I contacted his family to let them know what had happened and was soon joined by his sister, Eileen. We both sat with Joe for a while and he seemed to come around slightly. He began talking about the booking we had that night and how I should not disappoint anyone and play

records for them myself. I knew how to use the equipment since it was all our own and as I did not want to put any more strain on him I agreed to do it. He seemed a lot better after this. And so off home I went, leaving Joe with his sister, to prepare for my evenings work. Although I did not enjoy that evening, being busy did help it to pass quicker and I was able to make sporadic checks with the hospital on Joe's condition.

Luckily, no permanent damage had been done and he was soon home from hospital. The shock of it all had made him realise just how bad things were and we immediately began to discuss the possibility of moving. Joe began to put back on weight and obviously looked much better for it. His friends began to comment just how concerned about him they all had been and how they thought he had initially had cancer. The pursuing eighteen months was a battle of wills between myself and the entity in our home. However, its grip was never quite as tight again, as my head on confrontation with it often kept it at bay.

As time progressed the fortunes appeared to be smiling a little for us. Our house was put on the buyers market and, after what seemed like an eternity, eventually sold. An offer of radio work had come through for Joe, but it was on a station in Dublin, and so it looked like I would be going home. I didn't care where it was, as long as it was away from this house.

As the impending date of our move loomed closer, things began to go wrong again. Electrical equipment would break down for no reason; lights would switch themselves off, and even an ashtray cracked in front of us for absolutely no reason. The entity in the house was aware of our plans and was not at all happy about it. Part of the reason it was able to affect us all so much was because of our sensitivity to it and there was no way of telling if it would amass as much pleasure from anyone else living there. It did not want to let go.

On our supposed last day in the house, everything that could go wrong did. The removal van did not turn up, having broken down along the way. It was so late in the day that another one could not get to us in time and so we had to stay another night and wait for the original van to be fixed. We tried to make the best of things by re-connecting various electrical appliances, but found that none of them would work. We gave up and decided to load Joe's van up with the D.J. equipment and records that were in the garage. At this point, Alan was left alone in the house. He seems to recall the time in there alone extremely vividly, even though he was only eight years old. He described the atmosphere to me recently as "crushing" and recalled hearing noises, like that of furniture being moved, coming from our dining room which had been totally filled with our bedroom furniture. He recalled as he listened at the door, and eventually plucked up the courage to look inside. He told me that the room was not just dark inside, it was black, and even though he tried to turn on the light, it would not go on. After this Alan left the house and did not set foot in it again, spending the night as he did at his aunt Eileens, and to this day refuses to go near it.

Eventually, the removal van turned up and we loaded our belongings into it. We moved quickly and soon we were free of it. I will never forget the feelings of relief and elation as we drove away from it for the last time.

As we drove from Leeds towards the ferry port, our companion for all those years took one final stab at us. A green car spun out of control in front of us and we only just missed a collision. I remember the look of desperation on the young woman driver's face as she frantically fought to regain control of the car, which she had lost for no apparent reason. The wheel had simply jumped free from her hands, which caused us to swerve. Luckily, we were able to turn the car into a nearby garage forecourt, thus avoiding any harm. It was at this moment that Joe finally began to accept what I had been telling him for years about the manipulative energies connected to our house. He put his foot to the gas and we left Leeds behind as quickly as we possibly could. It was from this day that I had to accept that I would have to embrace my spiritual powers, as I was in no way prepared to ever go through such torment again. Even though I had tried for so long to shut them out, I now felt that they had grown to become such an important part of my life it was no longer possible to ignore them.

My second encounter with the spirit world.

My near death experience in my teens.

6

Home Again

It was good to be back in Ireland again. I felt very positive that things would be much improved on the times we had had in England and it was wonderful to be back in familiar surroundings and have family close by. We had been very lucky with the house we had bought. It was a beautiful three bedroom semi-detached located in an area called Kilnamanagh, which was just off Green Hills Road, a place that my mother would take us to pick field mushrooms and blackberries. The area was still beautiful, with greenery in abundance, and we had a magnificent view of the Dublin mountains from our back yard.

I was very fond of our new house. It was tranquil and warm and not at all like our previous home. Alan took to it straight away and immediately started to sleep with the light off in his new bedroom. It was a very happy house. Alan soon made new friends and settled down at school, which was just across the playing field at the back of us. Joe was busy playing records on a local radio station which was very popular in Dublin at the time. He was also resident disc jockey at several large city centre venues and proved just as popular here as back in Leeds. Things were going very well. In those days (it was the early eighties) I was very content to be a mother and housewife and enjoyed making our home beautiful. I was also able to spend more time with my mother, who had lived in England for a time herself, but had also returned home not long before we had. I also kept in touch with the friends I had in Leeds by telephone.

Joe's family were still mainly resident in Dublin and we often spent time with his three sisters and their families. His youngest sister, Tina, still lived with their father Maurice in the same house where the family had been brought up, and where Joe and I had spent time together years before. One particular day when we were visiting I was talking to Maurice. I forget the topic of conversation but as we were in mid flow I heard a whisper in my ear. It was Maurice's brother Ralph, who was by now in spirit. He told me to ask his brother where he was and why he had not been buried at his parents' grave site like he had asked to be. I got a strange urge to look up to the ceiling and, quite curious by his request, I posed the question to Maurice. "He's up in the attic", he replied, "I keep forgetting to bring him down and take him with me when I visit them." I then heard Ralph pipe up, "Well would you ever mind getting me down from there and put me where I'm supposed to be!" This was all just Ralph's way of letting his brother know that he was all right. He had probably been waiting a long time to get the opportunity to speak to Maurice and to finally have his request fulfilled! A short spell later, his wish was finally carried out and his ashes were laid to rest within a wooden casket alongside those of his beloved parents. We still hear from Ralph from time to time and he is always his same old cheerful self.

As time passed we became more settled yet some nagging thoughts began to disturb me. I started to get very strong impressions that we were going to be moving again, not to another house in Dublin, but back to Leeds. This greatly distressed me as I was still very aware of the terrible times we had gone through in our last house and I felt that if we returned to Leeds then all the effort we had put in to making this house our home would be wasted and the feeling of security we had established would be lost. I knew though that if it was indeed true, there would have to be a very good reason for it or I would flatly refuse to go.

One day shortly after I began to get these feelings, a stranger came to our door. She was a gypsy who was walking around the neighbourhood asking people if they could spare old clothes or food for her children as they were very hungry. I told her that I would give her what I could find in the way of clothing and whatever I could spare in food. I rummaged around a little and found some clothing that Alan had grown out of and a few tins and packets of food. She was very grateful for all this and I suppose felt obliged in some way to return the courtesy. Just before she left she stopped and said to me "I want to tell you that you will not stay in this house, no matter how much you want to. It serves its purpose at the moment but I must tell you that you have something to do elsewhere, something important. You have spirit with you and you will understand what is to happen when the time comes. When this happens you will be happy to go". At that moment I knew that it was inevitable that we would return to Leeds. I thanked the gypsy for her guidance and said farewell. I decided to make the most of my time here in Dublin as I knew now it wouldn't be a long stay. I got to know the city all over again by visiting all the important sights from my past. I remember going back to the Coombe and standing on the steps of the old hospital looking across at the new town houses that replaced the rows of flats we had all lived in. The steps were all that remained of the original building as it had been torn down some time ago. It had been an important sight for the city and I suppose leaving a little something of it standing was a way of paying respect to it. I was pleased about this because my mother had always elected to arrange the altar on the platform under the archway on the stairs. So this place was in my eyes, a tribute to my mother too as she used to put her heart and soul into those arrangements. I stood there and said a silent prayer for my mother. The new Coombe hospital had been built on Cork Street. This was at the back of the flats we had lived in after the fire. I had called at the old homes of many of childhood friends only to find, as I had anticipated, most of them had moved away. This was quite sad for me as it made me realise that things change and no matter how hard you might want something to stay the same it very seldom does. I was now quite happy to accept that I would have to go with the flow and welcome my future with open arms.

Of the few old friends that I had managed to re-establish contact with, there was one in particular that I became particularly close to again. Her name was June, and she lived quite near to Joe's father. We were having a cup of coffee one afternoon and we began talking about loved ones that we had lost to spirit. As we chatted, I noticed that June had a lovely little girl in a white dress standing beside her. The girl told me that she had passed over very suddenly and that June was a relation of hers. I told June about this. I also went on to tell her how upset the child's mother was and that she was pacing the floor with worry, but the little girl wanted June to assure her mother that she was all right and extremely happy where she was and had made lots of friends. June was ecstatic to hear all this and said that she only wished I had been there yesterday when the child's poor mother had been in her kitchen, pacing the floor in desperation at losing her child. June fetched a photograph of the little girl. She was wearing the same white dress I had described. Apparently the girl, June's niece, had passed over recently and no one had any idea why she had passed so suddenly. June assured both myself and the girl that she would relay her messages to her mother.

The next time I saw June she had indeed passed on the messages to a very relieved mother who was apparently much happier now she knew her child was safe and happy. As I once again engaged in conversation with her I announced that I had something more pleasant to tell her this time. I told her that I could see the Wheel of Fortune and that I could see her spinning it and winning! She was familiar with a game that was called by this name. I also described the area that this would take place and asked her if she recognised the description. She said "No" to this at the time but would keep an open mind. Some time later June spotted me walking up the street to Tina's and she called me in. "I have something to tell you" she remarked. "My friend won some money on "Wheel of Fortune". It's a game that moves around the city and is hosted in different areas. She asked me to go with her and spin the wheel for her because she was so nervous. Well, I did, Tress and we won. My friend even gave me some of the winnings as a reward for being so lucky!" She then explained how the place, which had in fact been in her locality, was exactly the same as the venue I had described. "I couldn't believe my eyes because I've been to that place so many times in the past and I just never thought of it." This was not the last time that I was to give June a helping hand.

Some time later, it was early summer, I was sitting with Tina and some friends in her kitchen. We were all having coffee and the conversation turned, as it seems to do around me, to how the spirit world offer help to us when it is necessary. For instance, I said to one of the girls "You are very aware of the fact that you can feel a presence. I know that you have a brother around you in spirit who took an overdose and it is him that you are sensing around you, even though he has been in the spirit world for some time now. He wants to let your mother know that he is not lost or wandering the Earth like a lost soul. He is with your father who has hold of him by the hand. He is content and smiling and is at peace. Your father lifted him." She said to me that her mother would be afraid to talk to me as she would be worried that I would have told her that he was not at peace. I explained to her that a cousin of mine passed on at the age of twenty-one, also from a drugs overdose. I knew very well that he was happy and safe in the spirit world. He had been off drugs for some time, but for some insane reason, had returned to them at a later date and taken the same sizeable dosage he was taking just before he had come off them. Hence he had involuntarily overdosed. Just as her brother had. When someone in that situation passes over, the priority of spirit is to help them resolve their problems and face their actions in order that they may live normal productive lives in spirit. I told her it was her brother's wish that his mother be informed of this but at the end of the day it was her decision whether or not she was told. Shortly after, the lady left.

A few days later I was back up at Tina's house and I found that the lady I have just spoken of had left word that her mother would like to talk to me and would I please call in, which I did. She wanted to say thank you to me personally. I told her that Tony was standing with us and her husband Liam was also here and that they were both blowing kisses towards her. She smiled at me and said that she was much more settled now that she knew he was at peace and united with his father. "I'm happy for you" I said as we parted. As I was walking back up to the family's house I bumped into

June. She was standing at her doorstep calling for her daughter to come in and have her lunch. She invited me in for a moment and we made some small talk about how Joe and Alan were doing as I didn't want to stay long. I was about to say goodbye to her and leave the house when I turned back. I said "I don't want to alarm you, but I MUST say this to you. And I must make sure that you do take notice, are you listening? There is going to be a very serious illness in your family soon. Whatever you do I must warn you not to let go. Do you hear what I'm saying?" June looked startled, but I continued "You must not give up at all costs. It will look very bad and you will be told to let go. Please take the advice that I am being told to give you as they will pull through. No matter what, they will survive".
A short while later, June's husband Tom took very ill and was close to passing. The last rites were given and the family were told that there was no hope at all. Everybody but June gave up. She kept hold of the message and kept repeating what I'd told her to the family. Everyone thought she was mad because she believed that someone from Heaven had told us that he would live. As I had stressed to her, he did not pass on and made a full recovery, much to everyone's amazement. Thank you kind messenger whoever you are, you truly were a blessing in disguise. June and Tom are a very united couple and I for one know that they have counted their blessings over the years since that time.

Faith

I lift up this pen and with its stroke
I open my heart to bring you hope
On the ground that we stand
Is a blessed land

God planted it firmly in our hands
Don't you see it's part of His plan
Unburden your heart, lift up your arms
Give it all up into His hands

He'll sort it all out with one mighty action
He gave you his word a long time ago
Have you not heard or did you not know?

I know this for sure, I asked Him you know
He just took my hand and it made my heart glow
I flew like a bird towards the promised land
As I stood there in awe I knew then His plan

He spoke to me softly and then He withdrew
He did not forsake me for I already know
He stood in my heart, His great plan for you
His strength is my armour, His breath is the dew

We had been living in Dublin for several months by the time all this had come to pass. My gift was growing stronger all the time and I was beginning to feel quite content and at ease with it. I felt very strongly that I was learning to control it more and, since I was older and wiser, would give more thought to the things I would say to people than I had in the past. I no longer 'put my foot in it' so to speak. I was much more forthcoming about my gift and did not hide the fact that I was able to communicate with spirit anymore.
There were developments in my personal life as well as my spiritual one as well by this time. Rather by chance, Joe had received word as to the whereabouts of his mother, who had left Ireland and lost contact with the family a long time ago. Joe had not seen his mother for over twenty years and the whole family were obviously very excited about seeing her again. Joe and his sister Eileen drove down to Coventry to

meet with her. It was a long overdue reunion and a thrill for their mother, Teresa, to see her children again after so long. It wasn't long before arrangements had been made for her to return to Dublin where she would spend a time staying with us before she set up home again on her own.

Joe's mother and mine had never met, and so we thought that it would be an enjoyable experience for both of them if they had dinner together. They soon began chatting together and it seemed like they had known each other for years. They both swapped childhood stories about us and talked a little about Alan, and then the conversation turned to spiritual matters and my gift. Joe's mother told of how I had brought her brother and sister through from the other side and many others, both friends and other family. From this, my mother began telling us about an experience she had herself that she'd never even told me about. She had undergone an operation many years ago, which had not gone smoothly and she had developed further problems. These problems were so severe that she had been given the last rites. She recalled how at one particularly critical point she had found herself on the ceiling looking down at her own body and the medical staff of the hospital frantically rushing around her, trying to revive her. All this while my mother was striving to get their attention and kept calling to them to get her down. She remembered being extremely frightened and confused as to why no one had noticed she was there. Dear God, she remembered thinking, don't let me die as my children are still growing up and they need me. She then recounted how she had heard a voice from nowhere speak to her "It's all right. You are not going to die and you are going back to your children". A calmness came over her and it was over. She had retained the entire memory when she was revived but had never spoken of it to anyone. When Joe heard this, he asked her why. "Because I did not understand what had happened, and I was afraid that people would think I was crazy". It didn't surprise me, as it was precisely the sort of thing my mother would not talk about. I often wonder what other experiences she has had that she'd never shared with us. She is a very psychic individual and I'm sure that this out of body experience is only the tip of the iceberg.

****

Although we had made many friends in Ireland and re-established links with family, I could tell that Joe was beginning to miss Leeds quite a lot. I knew that the time when we would return was drawing nearer with each passing day. I was waiting though for some word or sign from the spirit world that the time was right to make the move. Surely enough, one night whilst I was sitting alone in the lounge, my grandmother came to me. It was about one o'clock in the morning and I often liked to sit quietly by myself at that time. I was looking into the open fire, watching the embers die away before I put the fireguard on and went to bed. It was very comforting and cosy and I loved our open fire (the only thing I did not like was cleaning it out the next morning!). As I looked down at the ashes I was transfixed by what I could see. My grandmother was spelling out in no uncertain terms before my eyes that we would be back in Leeds within the next six months. I decided to keep this to myself as I wanted to see exactly how events would transpire.

About a month later, Joe brought up the subject of selling the house here and contacting some of his old venues in Leeds about the possibility of returning. The reaction was very positive to this and so I travelled over to Leeds and began looking at houses. I found a house, where Joe and I still live today, which was perfect for us. However, finding the house was the easy part, organising the complex move back was something else entirely.

I needn't have worried. I had faith in the message I had been given and everything ran like clockwork. The removal van which picked up our furniture had to make a delivery in London first and so everything was timed perfectly so that we got our furniture in the house on the day we moved in. Joe's work was lined up in advance and we had no trouble getting Alan into a new school.

I was sad to leave Ireland but excited at the prospects of the fresh start that awaited us. I knew in my heart that this time around in Leeds, our lives would be guided in a very different direction.

7

My Work Begins

Things had changed when we returned to Leeds. There was a completely different atmosphere around us and a strong sense of direction and purpose. I knew that the focal point of our lives was now going to be based around spiritual discovery and development and their implementation in the acts of helping others. It was to be extremely important work and we were told by our family in spirit that it would be very time consuming and we should be aware of this from the start. We had never lost touch with our friends, but I certainly felt that we had outgrown them in a spiritual sense, so both Joe and I accepted that we would not have very much freedom or leisure time, and that our priorities would be geared towards this greater cause.

My grandmother in spirit had begun to inspire me more and more as to the serious nature of my gift as she was very aware of just how involved my life would become intertwined in spiritual matters. I was also spending more and more time thinking about what Fred Moor had said to me many years before, about me taking my rightful place on the rostrum for spiritual work. I began going to these meetings again and, on one of my first visits, was amazed to find that I was given another message by the gentleman taking the service. He told me that my aunt, who had had chronic arthritis in life, had come along from spirit to say hello to me and tell me how pleased she was that I had stopped running away from my gift of mediumship. He also went on to tell me that she was showing him my name on a door that would relate to healing. "You won't go looking for any of this" he added, "it will all be brought to you by spirit. They will teach you how to use your gifts and you will use them for the benefit of all, even the animals of the earth". It was a little difficult for me to take all of this in at the time because it was a very overpowering message and I did not feel at all ready for this huge amount of responsibility that it seemed was to be thrust upon me. All I wanted to do was help the suffering in my own way, and whilst I appreciated the constraints that this would have on me I would have preferred my new role to be simpler, without lots of paraphernalia associated with it. The speaker could almost sense my thoughts and told me not to worry as I would be adapted over time to the fact that my gift would be used in a whole spectrum of ways and that I would be given signs as to how to do this.

I began thinking just what he had meant by "signs" and the more I thought about it, the clearer they became. For many years now I had been having a recurring vision. Sometimes it would greatly disturb me. I would be lying in bed ready for sleep when all of a sudden I would see the roof disappear and I would find myself looking at a group of men, women and children who were obviously starving and forlorn. As I watched them, I could see the hunger in their eyes and sense the sorrow in their hearts. It was very disturbing. After a few moments a phrase, rather like a chant, would commence saying "Feed these people". What I never understood was, since these people were from Third World countries, how was I supposed to physically feed them? We were barely making a living ourselves and so it seemed unlikely that we could offer much by the way of monetary support. I just did not understand, then, just after my experience at the church meeting, I had the vision again. This time I remember saying "Why are you showing me this when I am powerless to do anything about it? I'm tired of fighting this, it's in your hands. If I'm meant to help these people then show me what to do and I'll do it", and gracefully, I gave in. From that moment on, I felt as if my feet had been pointed in a new direction and I obtained an understanding of what it all meant. I was to feed these people (and anyone else so desiring) with spiritual food in order to sustain them in their times of need. I have never had the vision since, but the wheels were in motion and it was time to start putting things right.

It seemed that the first thing that spirit wanted me to do was to sort out a problem that I had been having for a long time now. They wanted me to deal with the condition that was causing me severe leg and back pains. I'm sure that some of you will have suffered with a bad back and know how excruciatingly painful it can be. I had suffered with this condition for many years now. Sometimes it would get so bad that I would have to spend days in bed recovering. The pain killers I was taking had kept getting stronger over the years and it seemed like the only way I was ever going to defeat it was to have a major operation. I had seen a consultant some time before and had been told that I had a trapped nerve behind my hip which was causing my back pain and the problems with my leg too. As spirit had been quick to point out to me, the work I was to become involved in would keep me on my feet a lot of the time and it was important that I be as comfortable as possible. I was instructed by my guide, Leao, and others from spirit who heal the sick and the dying, that Joe was to lay his hands on my leg and heal me. They were going to use him as a healing channel. That is not to say that it was to be a one off practice for my benefit only, but spirit felt strongly that Joe would be able to use his abilities to heal others in the future, too.

It took some time to convince him to try this as he doubted that he could heal me, but I was persistent and eventually he caved in. I relayed to him that he was to sit on the settee and that he should lift up my leg and put it across his lap. He then had to put one hand on my knee and another on my ankle. When he did this I felt an amazing sensation run through my leg. It was like a vibration that ran from one end to the other. After a few moments I felt my foot go numb as if it was being frozen. As we looked at my leg, we could see a rippling effect running down it. After a few minutes, we stopped and tried to produce this visual effect again ourselves but to no avail. It was a very strange experience indeed.

My leg felt very heavy and numb for a time after this, but as these sensations wore of I began to feel tingling from my hip right to the ends of my toes. I found it much easier to walk and experienced very little pain. I had one more healing session with Joe a few days later and my back and leg have been fine ever since. Joe was to heal me again on another occasion.

I had got up one morning and gone to pick something up off the floor. It accidentally fell from my hand and rolled under the bed. I stretched out to reach it and pulled a muscle in my neck. The pain was frightful. It ran right from my neck to the base of my spine. That evening it was so bad that I thought I was going to have to go to hospital with it but I heard my guide suggest that Joe give me healing. I was to lie on the floor on my tummy and allow Joe to kneel beside me and move his hands along my spine. I experienced a similar sensation as before and, thankfully, the pain subsided after a few moments. So once again, both Joe and my guide had come to my rescue!

It might be appropriate at this point to talk a little bit about healing and what 'healing' actually is. The term can be construed as having several meanings. Take, for example, a young child who has fallen and grazed his knee and comes crying to us. We pick him up, dry his tears, gently clean and dress the wound and cuddle him until he feels safe and secure again. We have restored the balance to his body and alleviated the shock to his system and the child goes off to play again. This is one form of healing.

If a child is doing badly at school and feels pressure on him to do better, it is wise to sit him down and discuss the issue with him. Talk TO him, not DOWN to him. The important thing is to make the child realise that they do not have to live up to the expectations of others, only to those of themselves. Some children progress faster than others and excel in different areas. If a child is told that they can only do their best and that is all that is required, then the healing process has begun and the child no longer feels threatened. If the mother brings a child to me to receive healing the first thing I do is talk to the child about their problems and let them tell me in their own time and in whatever way they choose. Taking this approach has very good results. The child looks forward to repeat visits and usually heals much faster because of their inner harmony.

We can all be down in the dumps from time to time. We may have had a bad day at work or an argument with someone close. Sometimes when we feel like this we can have the good fortune to encounter someone who has a good sense of humour or compassionate nature who will empathise with our feelings. they usually do or say something humorous or positive to cheer us up and we feel much better. This too is a form of healing. In fact, the greatest healing tool of them all is something we all have the ability to do in abundance, yet we very rarely do it, smiling.

Smile

Keep a smile on your lips for a while
And partake of the pleasure it brings
For a smile can bring with it an abundance of laughter
Which fills the gaps in the heart

So be a good soldier and wear a big grin
Let the harmony inside you shine through
For a smile can bring forth the ringing of angels
It's something you should not keep in

Why search for what's missing, it's better by far
To search for the truth from within
For God in His wisdom, if only you'd listen
Put what's in your heart for a reason

What I believe that poem from spirit is saying is that if we all smiled more and gave more positively from the heart, then we would all be much more enriched as human beings and the world would be a better place. Too often we ignore the whispering of the heart and allow negativity, instead of love, to go forth. Next time you see someone in the street or a friend who is upset, try smiling at them. You'll feel better and so will they!

There are other types of healing which you may not have thought of. The power of music is very strong for healing. Have you ever noticed that if you are depressed and you listen to an up-beat, happy song that your mood lifts with it? Or when you feel low and need someone to talk to that sharing a problem makes you feel better? Besides the instances I have outlined above, which are all within our grasp to master, there are other more specialised types of healing, including the kind that allowed Joe to heal me, that I will discuss a little now.

First of all, there is acupuncture. This is an ancient healing method which involves the use of pins on parts of the body (called pressure points meridians) to soothe the nervous system of our bodies. I do not practice this method but have seen the results that it can bring, and they can be spectacular. In rare cases it is used in operations in place of an anaesthetic. I have seen a video of such an operation where this was done. The operation was to remove a large steel pin which was about six inches long. The patient did not flinch and was fully conscious the whole time when the surgeons cut her leg open to remove it.

Another type of healing is called reflexology. This is a practice which, once again, involves the use of pressure points but only this time those located on the feet. The basis on which this kind of healing is based is that the various parts of the foot actually represent various other parts of the body, such as the heart, liver, lungs etc. I have not had very much experience with this form of healing but what I have heard has been quite positive.

The third type of healing which I want to mention is the kind I practice myself, which is spiritual healing. Spiritual healing is the laying on of hands, or in some cases, the hands are held over the body, just slightly, and guided around a particular area by spirit. The person involved must give their express permission for the healing to take place. This is called Free Will. If the healer continues without this consent then this is considered a violation of standard practice as you have taken away the persons right to choose.

This can make them feel insecure and vulnerable and can inhibit the healing process. I never give healing unless the recipient has had a medical check up. I firmly believe that it is in the patient's best interest because I feel that it is more beneficial for the type of healing I administer to work hand in hand with modern medicine, as opposed to working against it.

In order to help you understand how this type of healing works, I will need to explain about a part of your body which is seldom seen or talked about - the aura. The aura is an energy field which surrounds our body. It can be broken down into several layers of colour which each are assigned a particular characteristic of our personality, body and health. The first, outermost layer, is white in colour and is the layer furthest from the body. This layer is the spiritual layer and is the highest level in our aura. This level represents our spiritual awareness and is much stronger in those attuned to their abilities of healing and mediumship. The less aware you are in spiritual matters, the less developed and coloured this outer layer is.

The next colours inwards are silver and gold. These colours are intensified when we are in a happy, positive mood and relegated to a much poorer shade when we are fatigued or distressed. After these colours comes deep green (which I like to call God's colour). To me, this represents wisdom. It is intensified when the need for decision is paramount or if we find ourselves in any particular dilemma. It also can have a calming effect on the mind and is particularly attuned when in a rural environment. The next colours are pink, lilac and purple. These colours are very important as they are the primary healing colours and together help to regulate the general health of our bodies, as opposed to silver and gold which are more emotionally regulatory. Next in is the colour blue (which is at normality when it resembles the Madonna blue). A heavy blue in our aura usually means that we are disgruntled with someone or something and can often 'spill over' into the boundaries of our other colours, effecting our long term mood and sometimes health. Pale green follows the blue. In its ideal state, this colour represents harmony and contentment but, when we are envious or jealous of others it can become a much harsher shade and overshadow other colours, causing imbalance. Yellow is next and is another health colour. Usually this is a daffodil yellow but in times of ill health, especially problems in our internal organs, it can assume a much ruddier hue. Orange follows, which deals with the digestive system and helps our final colour, red, to supply our strength and energy. Too much red can signify anger, long standing illness or terminal health problems, such as cancer. Quite often the emotions associated with red are taken with us when we pass over, and it is then necessary for us to begin detoxifying ourselves on the spirit plain by exposure to more serene colours such as blue and green.

There is another part to our aura besides these outer colours. This is called the spirit aura. This is another band of white which closely hugs the body. It is not generally made visible to see as this part of our make-up is used as a storage space for all the things we do in our lives; it is our book of life. Whatever our actions, be they good or bad, they are stored here so that on the day of our passing we can review them and learn from them. We are held accountable to ourselves at this point for all our wrong doings but also rewarded for our good deeds, too.

Other colours can appear in the aura such as brown or black but these are normally present only in cases of extreme depression or suicidal tendency. Brown tends to be present when someone is fed up with their situation and feels there is no escape. The presence of black is significantly more serious as this causes major damage to our auras, which takes a great deal of spiritual healing and positive action to rectify.

When we heal the aura, we often concentrate on particular energy points around the body. These energy points are known as Chakras. It is these energy points that a healer goes to when they want to repair damage to the aura, which usually manifests itself in some physical symptom. In brief, there are seven primary chakras and six minor ones. Some spiritually aware people also have an eighth chakra which is situated to the right over the top of the head. This is called the psychic chakra.

I do not want to dwell too much on the intricacies of the chakras, as whole books on the subject have been written, but the basic principle of how they work is this. A chakra can be compared to two Catherine Wheels, which spin in opposite directions to one another. One wheel represents what we take in from the world and the other signifies what we give out from ourselves to our surroundings and other people. When these wheels are spinning at the same speed in the correct direction, the energy point is considered as balanced. However, as we go through our day interacting with others and generally muddling through the tasks of life, we encounter events which can upset the balance of these wheels, for example stress, tension, fear or frustration even an abundance of affection. These feelings cause the wheels to become imbalanced, not only between themselves but in relation to the other chakras too. If we are continually subjected to these forces the result is manifested in the aura as a severe disharmony of colours. If this persists, these problems spread into our physical bodies and become ailments, conditions and even diseases. That is why it is imperative that we maintain a positive and balanced outlook on life in order to preserve our energy and keep our colours balanced. It is when we let negativity take us over that our problems start.

It is possible to balance your own chakras or to have someone else do it for you. When you balance them you generally feel much more lively and alert. This can also aid in the recovery of illness or fatigue. There is a special section at the back of this book called Self Healing which explains in more detail how to do this.

Colours

Be meek in heart be meek in mind
Hold your anger from mankind
Still the form be slowly building
To douse the flames upon your shores

Though the boat it still be sailing
With its oars of brilliant gold
On its sails there is sky blue
Of the very brightest hue

Of the shade you call it yellow
See it sparkle and you will mellow
Of the green the deepest sea
Take from it and you will dream

And the orange it is well
Feel the warmth in you just swell
All the purple you can see
Take and hold it close to thee

Watch the blue and see it rise
As it spreads before your eyes
Hold it still and watch it spread
Now you know you have been fed

Now take the white, the purest white
And in it shines the smallest light
Don't let it flicker, keep it bright
Then you know you've filled with light

As I began my own self development, I chose to place a special emphasis on healing since I had asked for this special gift at my confirmation many years before. As such, I took whatever opportunities were available to learn more about the many different types of healing that exist in the world today. I would often go to healing seminars and look in wonderment at the displays and talk to people about their experiences and beliefs. One particular time I had been asked to attend a seminar near Roundhay Park in Leeds. It was to prove to be the first time that I used my gift of healing in a very profound way. I was sitting at a table writing out some spiritual poetry I was inspired to write. I was distracted from this when a lady came up to me and asked me exactly what spiritual healing was all about. I invited her to sit down and spoke about how I was made aware of my gift. I also felt a man's presence but could not see who it was, and so I brought this fact to her attention and asked her if she believed in life after death, to which she replied "Yes". I then told her that this gentleman was connected to her. I do not remember much else about the people I brought to her but I do recall being told to tell her that she had a long standing problem with her health and that she was experiencing a lot of pain in her right hand side. She was also quite amazed to hear me speak of the tests she had undergone and their lack of success at finding the cause of the severe pain she was suffering from it. I was asked by spirit to put one finger on the spot where the lady was feeling all her pain. I explained this to her and obtained her permission to proceed with their request. I told her that she was going to be healed. It was something that I could feel very strongly within my heart. As I felt this, I put the second finger of my right hand on her side. We both heard a loud POP! "That's it!" I said, "How do you feel?" I looked over at her and she was crying. "The pain has gone!" she exclaimed "What was that loud pop?" I honestly did not have an answer for that. She looked around the room and, catching sight of her husband, enticed him over and told him what had happened. She told me she had felt an overwhelming urge to come here this day as she felt a presence was guiding her by the hand in spirit. Her husband told me that she would pace the floor most nights because of the pain. We chatted a little while longer and they then thanked me and went on their way. It was a very worthwhile afternoon for me to know that I was able to help her and it remains strong in my memory to this very day.

I met this couple again some years later in Manchester at a similar event. They were overjoyed to see me as they had been to many such events in the hope that I would be there. I told them that I had been very involved in rostrum work and that on the day that we had met I had only gone out of curiosity to that particular seminar. She informed me that she had had no more pain from that day on and was going to make sure that she did not lose contact again. They have contacted me many times since. I even predicted that they would start up a business and it would go well. Several years on their business has blossomed and they have had to re-locate to expand it further. Even though I no longer hear from them, I often think back to that day with a big thank you in my heart for the instant healing my lady friend received.

As a healer, I have been bestowed with the added bonus of being able to see the aura that surrounds a person. I will never forget the first time I was shown it by spirit. I was at a church service at the Greater world, and sitting on the right hand side at the back, which was my usual spot, and I was very much drawn into the philosophical words being given by the day's guest speaker. She was in a state of trance, which some mediums can go into in order to communicate with the other side. Her voice had changed significantly from that of her own; it was a much deeper voice and spoke with a broken English accent although it was still clear what every word was. The tone seemed to transfix and relax me and as I listened I found my gaze being drawn away from the speaker and over slightly to the left hand side of her body. I became aware that there was a golden glow surrounding her that was stretching out from her body and dancing around the room. It was a magical sight. Standing next to her, but still within the aura, I could see a gentleman, turned sideways, wearing a smart suit and looking very regal. I was taken aback by this and quickly closed my eyes as I thought I must have been seeing things, but when I opened them again I found he was still there. He was obviously concentrating very hard on the speaker and I believe he must have been the source of her wonderful words.

I watched him throughout the lady's talk. When she had finished he stood back and moved out of her aura, that was when I lost sight of him. I was quite startled by the whole thing, but absolutely thrilled that it had happened. Unfortunately though, I had missed a large part of her talk through concentrating on her guide!

Being able to see the aura, which has since proven to be a very common occurrence for me, is of tremendous help when treating someone with ailments. I am able to look directly at their energy field and see exactly where the problems are and work specifically on healing those parts of the aura. Also, by looking at the aura it is possible to identify potential problems before they take root and quash them there and then, even before things are picked up on x-ray. There are books and articles on the subject of the aura, and something known as Kirlean photography, which can actually photograph it. You may want to look out for these things in order to enhance your understanding.

8

Influences & Progression

I very much enjoyed going to an open circle organised by the Yorkshire Spiritual Association (YSA) that was run in Leeds city centre. I found it gave me invaluable experience at directing my gift in more specific ways and a chance to talk to other spiritually gifted people. This was necessary as I still had to gain experience for myself and learn from other people. I became friends with a lady called Cheryl through one of these such groups and she briefly touched my life with her special qualities. We got on well from the start and soon were regularly attending church and circles together. She was spiritually aware although did not want to develop her gift in the same way I was developing mine; at least she had the choice about it, I did not!

Cheryl lived in an area in Leeds called Little London which was close by to the open circle we would attend. Quite often I would go to her flat before the service for coffee but I always had to insist that she meet me at a certain point as I often felt as if I was being stalked by someone or something as I walked through certain streets. When Cheryl told me about the area it was apparent why. She explained that the area had been named Little London because people in the past had often been snatched off the streets and never seen again. Folks would often walk around and stop to look over their shoulder from time to time. I found this quite morbid but understood that some sort of impression of the past had been left on the area which I was able to sense, rather like an atmosphere in an old house. I have always tried to avoid that area whenever possible.

One day, we were about to have tea at my house but just before we sat down at the table I was aware that a lady had joined us in the room and was calling my name. She asked if I could tell Cheryl that her great aunt Elizabeth was here. I held a mental conversation with her for a few moments and agreed to do this but I asked her if she could return after tea as I wanted the atmosphere to be just right when I spoke to Cheryl about it. She agreed to this.

After tea, we settled down in the living room and began chatting. I then noticed that Elizabeth had returned and was eager to be included in our conversation. I announced her by name to Cheryl. She immediately knew with whom I was speaking to and said "That's my great aunt". I was sitting beside the fireplace and began describing Elizabeth to her and also told her that she had placed a huge white globe of light up in the corner of the room at the other side of the fireplace for us. I watched Elizabeth walk around the room and stop in front of a large picture that was hanging on the wall behind Cheryl. Suddenly the picture fell from its hook and crashed to the floor behind, giving her a terrible fright. It was just Elizabeth showing us in another way that she was there and extremely excited that she had finally managed to get through to Cheryl after so long. It was a fascinating conversation, and Cheryl learned much about her family's history. We talked for a little while longer before Elizabeth announced that she would have to go but would leave the spiritual light for us to fade away over the next few days. With that, she was gone but her light did remain for a time.

After I had known Cheryl for a while, I began to feel very strong impressions about her future. I told her she would venture into politics; something which she very much doubted, but sure enough it came to pass. I've since lost touch with Cheryl but feel that she is doing very well for herself somewhere in England since she moved from Leeds some time ago. Her great aunt still drops by from time to time and so I learned that mediums do make friends in the spirit world as well as friends through meeting the family still here on the Earth plain.

****

I had met other people at my Monday group, too. The President and organiser was a very strong willed lady called Mary who put her heart into her role. She became a good friend and we have worked together on a number of charitable occasions. Also, I happened to meet a lady called Mrs. Hall who was to have a very strong impact on my life as a medium. She was truly one of the most gifted souls ever to walk this Earth. She told me much about what would come to pass in my life and was by and large correct on every count. There was a tremendous sense of trust and respect between us and I very much believed that we were old friends whose paths had crossed before in another time. Her influence, however, was not just restricted to me but also touched Alan as well.

As I have said before, Alan is very gifted spiritually and has often accompanied me to church meetings over the years. On one occasion, he encountered Mrs. Hall. She had never met Alan before and did not know who he was or even that we were related. This particular day she had approached Alan in the circle and spoken to him with a message. She announced that he was a very gifted soul and he would have a large spiritual role to play in later life and also proclaimed that he was in some way related to me and that one day we would work together. Alan had thanked her for her message and confirmed that we were in fact related and that there was a strong possibility we would work together in the future. This has come to pass as Alan and I have often collaborated on specific incidents involving clairvoyance and no doubt shall continue to do so for years to come.

On another Monday afternoon after the circle, not long after her message to Alan, we were having our regular cup of tea and a biscuit when she came over to me and gave me a little potted plant. I was very pleased with this as I knew it was very out of character for her as she had not been seen to do anything like this for anyone before. I think the reason she had gone to the trouble of buying me a gift was because of the message I had given her the week before. I had been told by spirit that she had a very strong fear that she would lose her eyesight, as it seemed to be a common occurrence in her family in old age. I simply had said to her that this would not happen and she would continue with her work for spirit for years to come with her eyesight intact, until she was ready to pass over.

Mrs. Hall was in her seventies when I had met her but had kept up her work for a long time. She crossed over a few years ago but still remains a true friend and returns to see me and my family once in a while and continues to share her wisdom and faith and can see for herself that her predictions have, and continue to come true to this very day.

The setting of this circle was also the site of a landmark experience for me - my first transfiguration. Transfiguration means that the mediums face changes appearance so that the recipient of the message sees the face of a loved one that has passed over. Sometimes it can be the whole body that is changed and even the voice can take on similar characteristics too. The medium's face is moulded to facilitate the shape and features of the entity in question. This might be a child or a woman or man, anything is possible. On this particular instance though, it was my grandmother who had appeared, in order to protect me from any strange beings, as I was still developing myself and it can be quite a traumatic experience for the body.

I was speaking to a lady in the circle and I brought a family member through from the spirit world. I can't remember very much about the message I gave her and probably would not have even recalled this incident had she not spoken to me after I had given her a the message and returned to my chair. She stood up and approached me and, sounding very excited, told me that she was puzzled as to why she had not seen me in the room before the circle had begun as she had looked for me in my regular chair but could only see an old woman there. She described the woman as partially paralysed down the side of her face and aged somewhere in her sixties and dressed in grey. It was this woman that had visually given her the message and she had only been able to see me after I had sat down again. She had never seen this lady before and had assumed that she was a new member when she had entered the room.

My friend was very thrilled by all this and kept thanking me for a tremendous experience as it was the first time she had ever seen a total body transfiguration. She asked if I knew who the lady who had appeared was and I informed her that it must have been my grandmother as she had suffered several strokes in later life and her face had been affected. Strangely enough, I was never aware that anything had actually happened when I gave the message as I did not feel a thing. It is a pity no one had a camera as I'm sorry I missed it!

As time went on, other people in various groups and meetings I attended were aware of similar transfigurations and would often share this with me, each and every time though I had been unaware and I still wait for the day when I will be able to see this wonderful phenomenon on somebody else, so spirit, you have been asked!

My spiritual gifts were progressing and developing in other ways, too. I was becoming very aware that I had an ability to channel spiritual energy from pen to paper in the form of automatic drawing and writing (such as the poems which illuminate this book). Automatic drawing can depict anything, it really depends on whom the spirit involved is and what they wish to communicate. One evening, I was informed by my guide that I was required to do this and I should prepare and assemble my implements for the task.

Joe was visiting his sister Eileen at the time and Alan was upstairs in his bedroom listening to records, leaving myself and our dog, Solo, settled in the living room. I had started to draw and it was developing quite nicely. The picture emerging was of my guide, Leao. As I drew I noticed that I had been joined in the room by two familiar figures, both nuns who regularly visit the family. Our dog was looking at them in wonderment and kept tilting his head and wagging his tail as they came and stood beside us. I finished my drawing, said a prayer of thanks and moved across the room to where I could watch Solo who was still reacting to the nuns. Some time later, they left the room and our dog walked across to me. The next thing I heard was Alan's footsteps come bounding down the stairs calling out to me to come upstairs and watch the light show in his room! Alan recalled "I was lying on the bed listening to a Madonna record and I had the lights off because it was quite late. I looked up into the room and saw dazzling globes dancing around and giving a coloured brightness to the room. I watched this for a while before my attention was drawn to the end of my bed where I saw a nun standing, or rather floating. She seemed to acknowledge me and then turned about and disappeared through my bedroom wall. It was quite shocking as I was not expecting anything like that to happen. I wasn't frightened, I was probably more excited, and I ran downstairs to tell you". When I reached Alan's room everything had returned to normal. Alan had not known what I had been doing in the living room and so I told him about the two nuns visiting me earlier. I suppose they just wanted to say goodnight to him and give him something to watch to accompany his Madonna record! They certainly had a sense of humour.

Solo is no longer with us now as he was killed in a road accident after breaking free of his lead when he was ten months old, but our dear nuns look after him in spirit and often bring him back to see us.

Solo

Solo you were a little rascal
A wee small ball of fur
Your coat was silky black and white
The first week you kept us up all night!

Many a shoe went in the bin
You would chew the sole and then the skin
And the heels around the brim
Then you'd look at us so melancholy

You seemed to grow up overnight
Those big dark eyes which caught the light
Were closed forever one sad night
As you broke free to cross the road

As a car came speeding by
And you were hurt, we heard your cry
We rushed and held you in our arms
But the choice was down to you

As we laid you down to rest
I looked at you and said "Goodbye"
Our eyes they seemed to say
You know that we will meet again one day...

Losing Solo was a blow to all of us as losing a dog can be like losing a family member. Some people think it is silly to grieve for an animal but I can assure you that it is not. They become integral parts of our lives and can have a profound effect on us. We were given another dog after Solo, which we named Chewie. He was small and thin but had a very loud bark and perfect German Shepherd features even though he was a cross breed. Sadly, he was not meant to stay with us here on the earth plain either, as he was suffering from parvovirus when we got him. He lived one short, painful week with us, but stays remembered in our hearts forever. Our third dog, was called Tulsa. We had Tulsa for eleven wonderful years before he left us for spirit in the summer of 1997. Do please remember though that animals thrive in the spirit world and are re-united with us when we pass, so don't despair if you have lost a pet as they do still visit you and will be ready and waiting for you when it is your turn to cross!

****

As I've already established, I was learning to use my gift in many different ways. Many of these ways were natural and instinctive to me but there were also instances where spirit pushed me into finding ways of using my gifts in very exceptional and sometimes disturbing situations.
I was informed by my guide, Leao, that the time was coming when I would be used in what is known as rescue work. This is where a medium goes to a location, be it a home or a piece of land, and attempts to establish contact with a restless spirit or spirits who are causing disruption and ask them to move on. Usually the medium actually has to guide them over as the reason they are restless is because they have lost their way to the light. This is, of course, a classic Yin and Yang situation, though sometimes the spirit concerned knows fully well what it is doing and where it should be going to, but chooses to ignore it. It remains purely for it's own satisfaction because it finds pleasure in distressing others. This was probably the case with the spirit in our first semi-detached home some years before.
The phone call came at around 10:30 pm on Christmas Day in the mid-eighties. It was a lady called Marion, from one of the church groups I attended, and she was very aggrieved. She told me that her son, his wife and children were all hysterical and had fled from their home, sought refuge with her and were refusing to go home. I told her to get the children settled in bed and I would call her back in a few moments, which I did in due course. From this point I was able to establish that there had been strange events occurring in the house in question for some months now, but for some reason in the two weeks before Christmas, they had become much much worse. The family had already contacted the local church but were still waiting for the Vicar to make a visit. Since the family had already contacted someone, I did

not feel it was my place to interfere and so I told Marion to keep me informed and that I would ask for spiritual help for the family and, if all else failed, then I would be willing to help.

A couple of days later I received a phone call from Marion's son, Raymond. He told me that no one wanted to help his family and the Vicar had refused to visit their house. They had fled the house again and were not prepared to go back. They had left everything switched on and not even bothered to lock the doors and windows when they left, such was their dilemma.

I agreed with Raymond that Joe and I would come out to the house that afternoon and that he and his wife should pick us up. I felt very strongly that his wife Lisa attend with him as I knew that she had a large part to play in what was happening. My guide informed me that she had opened dimensional doorways in the house (rather like pulling back a dividing curtain which has us on one side and the spirit world on the other). When this happens, it acts like a beacon to the other side and attracts all kinds of things. Whatever events had transpired around this lady in the last few months had somehow caused this to happen.

As I approached the house in the car, I could sense that there were specific areas in the building that were specific to the problem; the kitchen; the cellar and the master bedroom. I could also sense a presence connected to the family, a man who had committed suicide, although he was not the source of the disturbance. I told Raymond's wife to remain in the car and I would call her in when the house was clear. She seemed to settle with this as it gave her hope.

I got out of the car and walked toward the house. Its vibrations expanded from the house into the garden and I could well understand why the family had become so frightened of being here. I went inside. The cold chill in the air instantly hit me in the face, yet the central heating had been on for days and had not been switched off when the family left. The first room I decided to visit was the kitchen as I knew it was not empty. As I pushed the door open, an old lady appeared before my eyes in front of the window. She looked troubled and started to point to the kitchen floor, getting more and more upset as she did so. I turned to Raymond and asked him if the house had been extended since they had moved in to which he answered "Yes, the kitchen was an extension that we added". Once I had established that this room was not part of the original house the old woman seemed to perk up and drifted in front of us and down into the cellar. I followed her down. She moved across to the wall at the far end and pointed at it. She then spoke to me and explained the reason for her lament. This part of the cellar and the kitchen above it were part of her old home that had backed on to this house many years ago and had been torn down and left as waste ground. When I re-iterated this to Raymond he confirmed this and said they had been granted planning permission when they moved in to build the kitchen. I realised that the lady was upset because nobody had thought to ask her permission to build on the land which she still felt was hers to dwell on. She had not realised that she had passed on. She had tried to get the family's attention by making banging noises, but to no avail, and the situation had just grown worse through their ignorance to it all. I told the lady that she no longer belonged here and that her family were standing by her side, waiting to welcome her into her new home through the light. I asked her to turn to her right so that she would see them and she did, with her husband and mother falling into her view. As her husband took her hand I watched them go

forward and wished them peace, love and light. As they left, the temperature began to rise quite noticeably.
We left the cellar and proceeded upstairs to the other location I felt strongly about - the master bedroom. I knew that whatever was in there was not particularly friendly and was the major source of the families troubles. As I stepped inside I was overcome with a feeling of anger which washed over me and seemed to lay stagnant in the room. Raymond's wife had been pulled from the bed on a number of occasions in here and had been having a great deal of trouble sleeping due to this oppressive force. As I walked across the room, I saw through its mask. It had been pretending to be the family's friend who had committed suicide a few months ago and Lisa had obviously taken to it, which gave it an excuse to stay around, extracting enjoyment from its torments. I spoke to the entity and told it that we knew it was an impostor and it would gain no more pleasure here so it should leave and go in peace and into the light. We argued for some time before it relinquished its control over the house and skulked away. As it left the heavy weight in the room lifted and the hot air that had been held back for so long swept into the room like a hurtling stallion and all was well again. We prayed together for this sad individual, that he find peace and happiness. We now brought Lisa into the house, and the four of us sat in the living room in a circle sending our positive thoughts and blessings into the house. I then blessed the rooms of the house. As an added protection, I also put salt across the threshold of every door. It seemed that Lisa had been very shaken by their friends suicide and was dearly missing him. She is a very psychic individual but was unaware of this at the time and ignorant to the fact of just what she had attracted. Thankfully though, the family have never been bothered again.

Although hauntings are rare, it was not the only instance I encountered in the early days of my development. Spirit deemed it a necessity for me to sample as many different experiences as possible. I think that I was led to these experiences as part of my spiritual growth. One Saturday, I was at a hotel in Pontefract, West Yorkshire, demonstrating my mediumship. It had been a very long day and I found I had been plagued throughout the day by a presence who I felt had been connected to the building in the past, possibly a maid or cook of some description. At the end of the day, I stopped the landlady as she walked through the main hall and engaged in conversation with her as I was most curious as to whom this presence was and why I felt so strongly about seeing certain areas of the building. As soon as I began talking to her, it became apparent that she was aware of the presence I was referring to. I pointed up at the ceiling, which was domed, and asked if I could be taken up there as I felt that it was an area connected with the entity in question. I followed her upstairs to a part of the building that was rarely used and was not properly wired with electricity so we had to bring a torch. I had to lead as the landlady did not like venturing up here alone and she would not go up there any other way. When we had climbed the stairs, I found that there was a doorway to the room in which the dome was located. I didn't want to go into this room, though, as I felt that I would be trespassing and not showing the proper respect to whatever energies had chosen to exist in there. I also knew that this was not the room that I wanted to visit. I felt I should have been at a higher, older level in the building and the dome was a fairly recent addition to the hotel's design. When I told this to the landlady she was very relieved that we were not going in as she didn't like the room. She explained that it was always locked and only herself and her husband had access to the key, yet every morning when they checked the door, it would be unlocked and open. I didn't think this strange since the tremendous energy behind the door probably didn't like to be grounded and captive.

I asked her if there was another room any higher than this, as I could see an old room which had no plastering on the walls and was very much a shell, with some light from a small window which looked over a courtyard. I could see this room was neighboured by a slightly larger, much darker room which had no natural source of lighting at all. She told me there was such a room but she had only been there once and found the atmosphere very frightening and distasteful and would not go up there again. I eventually persuaded her that she would come to no harm as I would be with her, so she begrudgingly agreed and went to fetch the keys for this sinister room.

When she returned we walked down along the corridor to another locked door which, when opened, I found was adjacent to a small set of stairs leading upwards. We walked up to the first room which was as black as night as I had described. the smell was of age and decay and we very delicately crossed the floor with only the light of our torch. The poor landlady was practically holding on to me for dear life with fear. I, on the other hand, was overwhelmed with sadness and loneliness of a woman who had once frequented these quarters. She must have suffered a terrible loss. The impression of these emotions was very strong in the room and were probably imprinted there many hundreds of years ago, since this building was extremely old and this part of it had not been modified or used since that time.

We moved slowly on towards the closed door at the end of the room. You could have cut the atmosphere that flowed from the room with a knife. I knew that this was where I wanted to be. When we opened the door and stepped inside I found it was exactly as I had described - a bare shell with a tiny box window. This is where the lady chose to remain, alone and in pain. I touched the naked brick wall and said a prayer for the unfortunate lady and urged to seek peace and move on. I can only assume that I was shown this room as the lady had wanted to share her pain with someone and have them acknowledge and remember that pain and suffering were here and those that had experienced it should not be forgotten. I felt very strongly that this area should have been marked as a memorial sight of some sort and that it should not be altered or used in any way.

After a time we left that room, which was the heart of the building, I felt I wanted to move on. My impressions now were of the bowels of the building in the cellar and so I requested I be taken down and shown it. Thankfully, the landlady complied with my wishes. As we walked down, she explained how strange voices were often heard in the corridor to the cellar and in the kitchen just above it. She also recounted how the kitchen staff would sometimes hear noises like pots and pans being moved about, only at the time they had always been put away or hung up.

I found that the cellar was very well lit as it was used for beer storage and so there were frequently people down here. I looked around a little and immediately saw two large archways in front of me, imbedded in the wall and sealed up. I told the landlady that there were many more arches like these connected by tunnels which ran around the entire area. I also felt that we were standing on some kind of water source, possibly an underwater stream or a well. The land lady was adamant that nothing like that existed down here. We continued to explore the cellar, which she did not venture into very often as she did not like this area either, and found a small door that she had not encountered before. When I asked what was behind it she opened it and looked inside. When she had done, she looked at me, quite ashen faced, and said "Tress, I owe you an apology. There is a well in that room built into the floor." I looked inside and it was indeed true, there was my water.

I opened myself up further at this point in order to grasp the relevance of this room to the puzzle. As I looked back at the archways I could see people walking through them as if using the tunnels to move around the town. Some of the people were soldiers dressed in very archaic clothing, whilst others resembled old English peasants who had been brought together for some reason, possibly for breaking some law. It was then I felt the pain and fear which I could associate with that in the top room, so whatever had happened down here must have had some bearing on the lady upstairs.

I explained my feelings to the landlady who asked if I knew anything about the history of Pontefract to which I replied "No." She told me how in Medieval times the whole area was a mass of catacombs which were used to get up to and out of the church which was at the bottom of the square. There had been some fighting in these tunnels in the past which had inevitably resulted in bloodshed. In later years, all the tunnels had been closed off and converted into cellar space for the many homes and premises of newer buildings built in Pontefract. You may be able to seal these tunnels, I thought, but you cannot seal up the psychic energies left behind from a time so long past.

****

All these encounters and meetings were moulding me and

helping me to develop. I do not regret anything that has happened in life as I feel all of my life's events were necessary to determine my character and my work. It does hurt to loose loved ones but the wonderful thing about the gifts I have is that it offers comfort and hope, not just to me but to others, too. It can help ease the suffering of those still living with us through healing and appease the friends of relatives of those who have passed on through clairvoyance. We are never ever truly separated from our loved ones, it's just like being on opposite sides of a curtain, as I illustrated earlier, it's just that most of the time that curtain is closed so as we can only have partial contact. It is just a pity that more people are not aware of the joys and comfort that can be found for both us on the earth plain and those in spirit. I knew that it was my task to help enlighten these people, which is why I took my next step - onto the rostrum.

9

Speaking Out In Public

Many spiritual centres and churches regularly hold special events to raise funds during the year as well as running their regular demonstrations. As time progressed, I found that I was becoming involved in both of these.
My work on the rostrum has taken me all over the country and in to parts of Ireland, too. At first it was quite a daunting experience for me since it was something that I had maintained I would never do when I was younger, yet here I was practising my mediumship in front of large groups of people just as Fred Moor had predicted. I became more relaxed over time and found myself enjoying these evenings a great deal. It was also nice to have the opportunity to help a larger number of people than was possible in an open circle and it also gave me a chance to promote the spirit world to the many who attended these services out of curiosity.
Sometimes I became involved in special evenings organised for specific groups of people such as the terminally ill. One such evening took place some years ago in the neighbouring city of Bradford. I was approached by an organisation of nurses and asked if I would like to attend one of their regular weekly meetings which were held to help the terminally ill and their families come to terms with their situation. The

aims of the group were to illustrate the positivity of making the most of their time remaining and to help them overcome their fear of death. They were keen for me, as a spiritual medium, to give a talk on life after death and also try some spiritual healing. I was delighted to accept their offer and went along the following week to their meeting.

The group met on Wednesday evenings in a room that was donated free of charge by a hotel in Bradford city centre. As soon as I had stepped into the room I could feel how strong the atmosphere was, but it was not depressive. Instead the room had a very warm, cosy feel to it and there was a very high energy level there. I could sense that people were curious about me and who or what I was. I knew I would have to present my demonstration in a very tactful and balanced way as I didn't want to upset anybody. My intention was to instil confidence in them and open their minds to the possibilities of what exists beyond our physical bodies not to terrify them and offend anyone's religious views!

I began by giving an overview of my beliefs and talking a little about myself and about the proof I had been given regarding life after death. I explained about my own out of body experiences and the peace and tranquillity they had lead me to experience. This seemed to trigger a reaction from the group and soon the room was resounding with discussion. One gentleman broke through the noise to ask if I could see spirit, to which I replied "Yes". He then asked if I could see anyone standing with him. I knew that this was a test for me. I looked at him and could see a gentleman standing behind him who revealed his name as Gerald. I told my questioner about this man and also that he had only just passed over. He seemed satisfied at this as it had indeed been the case. This seemed to offer some comfort to others in the audience who had recently been bereaved and I soon found myself being asked if I could see or speak to specific members of families. I explained that I could not guarantee to bring anyone through as that is down to the spirit in question if they want to speak and whether or not my guide in spirit will allow them to come through to me.

I noticed a couple in the audience who I felt had suffered a great loss and I was not surprised at this point that they asked me about their young daughter who had left them after a long struggle. I dearly wished that I could have offered them the comfort of communicating with their beloved little girl but I knew that her suffering in this life had been so intense that it was going to take time for her spirit to heal and thus it would be some time before she could be brought through to them. I did tell them, however, how they would know that she was close by and would reveal herself to them in time. With that, I felt that I was able to move on to my next topic of the evening which concerned the aura.

I began explaining how I am sometimes able to pick up conditions that people are suffering with. By this I mean I can often physically feel the pain or discomfort a person may be experiencing due to illness or injury. Sometimes these problems can manifest themselves within the aura. They reveal themselves as contrasting colours around the inflicted part of the body, thus allowing people such as myself to see where the problem lies. Once again, this topic aroused some hearty discussion and a lady on the front row directed a question about this to me. She asked if I could see any health problems that might be visible in her aura. I looked carefully at her for a few moments to see what I could see and then conveyed my findings. I could see that she had a problem with her shoulder and arm; something that had been there for quite some time. She smiled at this as it was indeed true and explained how this problem had been with her throughout most of her life and meant that she had to put strain onto her good arm which was a considerable amount since she was a nurse. I was pleased that I was able to illustrate my talk with examples and thanked the lady for sharing her problem with the group.

By this time I had been standing for over three hours and was growing tired, but no one in the room had shown any sign of wanting to leave and so I continued. A number of people were asking questions and one which was repeatedly been touched on was the subject of burial. I explained that it did not matter whether you were buried in the ground or cremated, the spirit within us all goes on no matter. The shell remains left behind because it is no longer needed, but the spirit takes on its own physical form on the next plain and they are as real to the touch there as you and I here. I elaborated on the funeral service itself by saying that we do not remain within the coffin but are much more likely to be standing by the graveside with our family and friends watching the event ourselves and wondering what all the fuss was about!

I have found through experience that many people who attend the evenings of clairvoyance that are open to the general public are those suffering recent bereavements and are looking for some confirmation that their loved ones are all right. I remember a very touching incident at an evening in Leeds more recently. I had been directed by a young lady to a woman in the audience as I had to express her thanks for the blue and purple flowers that she had put on her grave. I gave her this and told how the young lady was healthy and very happy in her new life. I could tell this girl had been about seventeen at time of passing and the woman I was addressing was her mother. She wanted her mum to know that she loved her and was now with her friends, but that it was her that had been her best friend. I then asked the woman who Carol was to which she replied "That is my name". She spoke of how her daughter Emma had passed in her late teens very suddenly. I felt very strongly that this was due to a brain haemorrhage as I was developing a strong pain in my head. Carol confirmed that this was indeed correct and asked me to continue. I wanted to remind her about a scarf that was an important part of her life and was not surprised to hear that the scarf around her neck was something she wore always as it had belonged to Emma. Sensing that I still needed to speak with her, as I could feel that she was in desperate need of spiritual healing due to her trauma, I asked her to remain at the end of the evening which she seemed happy to do, and I continued with the demonstration as it is important to give as many people as possible something to take home with them. I am pleased to say that after that evening and through the many times I went on to see Carol for private healing, she is much better now and at peace with her daughters passing. As for Emma - she is chasing rainbows in a place far better than you or I.

****

My work in this area has lead me to uncover a very special gift that I had not really experienced before. One night I recall being told by spirit that I should sit quietly with a pen and paper, as I had often done for psychic drawings. They told me that I was going to start writing down information that was to be given to people I would meet at seminars or do readings for in the future. I found this quite amazing that I should be expected to write out readings for people in advance, especially when I hadn't the faintest idea of who these people were! But then again, I know now I should never question the capabilities of spirit. After all, if spirit can give me a message to pass on to someone on the phone around the other side of the world, surely they can see who I'll be meeting in the future!

The information I was given was clearly meant for several different people as I was instructed when to start a new page. Spirit had me put the time and date on the paper and on this first instance, instructed me to keep them until I took an evening of clairvoyance in Pontefract.

When the evening came around some weeks had passed. It had grown deadly cold and I couldn't tell whether it was warmer within the building or outside! The rain was thundering down and there was a rush to get inside. As people began to gather in the hall, they clumped together for warmth. It was more like a scene from a Dickens novel than a clairvoyant evening!

As I began I remembered that I still had these pieces of paper in an envelope waiting to be used until such time as spirit told me to remove them and go to the people they were intended for. They would give me little clues, like the colours they would be wearing, and I would seek them out. The time eventually came and I found a lady who seemed to match the clues. She was seated to the left two rows back and so I was able to reach her quite easily. I started to go through the information on one of the sheets of paper; it outlined events such as birthdays and bereavements and also several names. Two of the names, Terry and Jim, she could not place. I tried to help her by saying that Jim had passed not long ago but Terry was still very much alive and well and that she would have her memory jogged by them sooner than she would expect. She nodded to me and said that if this did indeed happen she would find a way of letting me know.

Some time later I was to meet this lady again, who I know now is called Janet, at another gathering in Pontefract. She approached me very excited and recounted her story. She harked back to the night of the clairvoyant evening and recalled how the heavy rain had forced her and a companion to seek refuge in a nearby pub to escape the downpour. They had a considerable distance to walk back to their car and decided that they might be best to wait a while for the rain to pass over. She told me that she had barely walked in the door of the pub when she was approached by someone she knew that she had not seen in a very long time - Terry! As she had greeted him she asked how his father was, who she remembered to be called Jim. Terry woefully told her that his father had unfortunately passed on only a few weeks before. The lady admitted to feeling quite shocked at all this and quickly told Terry about her earlier experience with myself and produced the piece of paper with the names on. As they had continued to talk they realised that all this must have been a sign from Jim to his son that he was still around and not to worry. Terry was thrilled with this news.

These events confirmed to everyone concerned that there is indeed more to life than this physical existence we know and it is through events like this, engineered by spirit, that help to show the many people out there who still have a doubt in their minds just how real the next world is. Janet only attended the evening out of curiosity but the ramifications of the nights events convinced her of life after death and proved to have a knock on effect to others around her, too.

I still use these "pre-readings" quite regularly and have diversified this gift into doing postal readings too. They are, however, merely a tool that I have to work with as the information given to me still comes clairvoyantly and is simply transferred to paper. It is one of many such tools that

I can use in my work alongside psychometry (clairvoyance through holding specific objects); cards; runes; gemstones and the crystal ball. Which leads us on to another interesting story.

It might first be prudent to explain what a crystal ball is for. It is a prop which I do not have to use but sometimes do since it holds a certain fascination with many members of the public. Within it I can see pictures - both animated and still, of things in the past, present and future. These things might be anything from some important location to illnesses my sitter may be suffering from. If, though, I chose to look away from the crystal I would still be able to see these things as I am the receptor for these images and not the crystal.

This particular story took place at a seminar in Burnley near Manchester. A lady had dropped in and asked the doorman if anyone within the room could see into her crystal ball which she had been left in a will. One by one the demonstrators in the room were asked to look into it and see if they could detect anything but to no avail. The lady was about to leave, quite unhappy that she had not accomplished anything when someone suggested I be shown it. I was talking to someone at the time but when I was free I approached the lady and took the ball from her. I gazed within it and saw several pieces of information comprised of imagery and names. One of those names was that of the person who had left it in her will. The lady was delighted that someone was finally able to fulfil her wish and I am pleased I was able to confirm for her that crystal balls do indeed work. They do have a more serious side however.

Several years ago I had arranged with the president of the Yorkshire Spiritual Association (YSA) to do a different kind of evening of clairvoyance which we call "specials". On this type of evening a divine service is held alongside philosophy, prayer and hymns. After this, the speaker of the day takes to the rostrum for a demonstration. These are events for which there is a door charge, which helps keep our spiritual institutions going. I enjoy these specials because they are my way of saying "thank you" to spirit for granting me the gift of healing and so I provide my services free for the evening. It is unfortunate that whilst our churches are recognised by the Government they receive no funding from it and as such have had to become a registered charity. I would urge you to support your local church as much important work is done there. The doors must be kept open so those in need of healing and help have a place to find it.

This particular evening was different from others I had done at that time in that my guide Laeo had instructed me to bring along my crystal ball for the evening. I thought at the time that this was quite unusual as we do not use them in church.

The night went along very smoothly and peacefully and just as I was finishing my last message my guide reminded me to remove the crystal from its covering. I told the audience that I was going to show them the crystal ball and asked them if they would like to touch it. I was not surprised to see nearly everyone in the room put their hand up!

I was very drawn to hand it firstly to a lady at the side of the room and so placed it gently into her outstretched hands. I then looked within it and gave her a message from one of her family. I had brought her husband through, who had been in spirit for some time, and he told me that I should give her the name Harold as it was been presented within the crystal. The woman stared back at me in total wonderment and told me "I have been waiting for this day for the last 20 years as I was always asking for his name when a medium brought through a message from him. One time he told me through a medium that he would give it to me one day and that day would come when I held a crystal ball in my hand and not before then".

"As I was getting older I had begun to think that day would never come when I would hold one of these so this has left me with no doubt in my mind that my husband will be there waiting for me when I pass over. He has kept his promise. Out of all the people in this room you came to me and I truely believe it was spirit that moved you." She ended "You have made me a very happy lady and I will never doubt spirit again thanks to you and that wonderful crystal ball of yours".

I had always known that one day I would possess a crystal ball and recall speaking of it many years ago to my friend Josie. It is not something I would have gone out and bought myself though. you can imagine my surprise then when I unwrapped a rather heavy Christmas present from Joe, to find one inside, especially since I had never spoken to him about them. It just goes to show how spirit move in mysterious ways!

10

Sittings And Such

As the 90's rolled around I found myself concentrating more on healings and special evenings of clairvoyance and less on the seminars I had been attending for so long. I very much wanted to establish a base of my own where people could visit me for both healing and readings. It was to take me a good year before I had found myself a room in Leeds city centre which was accessible to all and adequate for my needs at that point.

I must admit that it certainly was a nice change not to have to do so much travelling since both Joe and I had spent the majority of our time attending seminars around the country in the last few years. It also meant that I was able to establish more of a relationship with those who would come to see me for healing, since they were able to come back more regularly without making an excessive journey. Add to this the potential for finally starting a regular development group of my own and you have one very happy medium.

Initially, I shared a centre, which meant I only had a very limited amount of time and space there, but it was the foothold I needed and something to build on. I soon discovered that word of my whereabouts didn't take much time to travel since I was already quite well known in the psychic circles of the area and people talk. I became very busy indeed and Joe was rushed off his feet organising times for people to attend for healing and readings. Sometimes though, people simply call out of curiosity to find out exactly what I would be doing for them if they came to see me at my centre for a consultation, or sitting, as I prefer to call them. I will endeavour to explain this a little to you now.

Firstly, I try to make sure the person having the sitting is feeling comfortable. I explain that I am a spiritual medium and that I receive advice for them from their loved ones in spirit. These spirits are usually friends or relatives who simply wish to give a little proof to us that the afterlife exists. I also explain about guardian angels, who may wish to communicate more directly with us and often these guides choose to reveal themselves to me by appearing within the sitter's aura. Guides usually stand to the back of us on our left and can be men; women or even children (My own guide, Leao has the most beautiful dark flowing locks and wears a transfiguration white tunic with a red cloak that just touches the ground). The sitting then begins.

There are several different methods that spirit use to convey their messages to me. The first is by inflicting an illness or emotion on me that the sitter can relate to. This I have spoken about previously and it is called a condition. Sometimes it may be a condition of the sitter themselves but usually it is an impression of something felt by a loved one who has passed. The type of condition and how I relate it to the sitter, indicates who that person in spirit is. For example, I might feel a chest pain or slight paralysis which could indicate a heart attack or a stroke.

Another more common way is to be shown a picture of something in my head, perhaps a new baby or a special place. I explain the image to the sitter and try to establish an interpretation with them. This is known as clear seeing or clairvoyance. Similar to this is clear hearing which is a term used to describe the voices one might hear out loud or inside your head. The voice might say something like "tell him Ralph said hello" or give dates; names; places and so on by which to identify them. Sometimes they will be very direct and just give you their name! Although it has been my experience that most people in spirit like you to work a bit harder than that.

The number of people who come through during a reading varies considerably. Sometimes there may just be a few spirits in the room with us or, on the other hand, the room may be completely full! Also, it is often the case that someone who passed on before you were born or a person you never met is brought through. I will usually instruct the sitter that this person has always known them; watched them grow up and develop. They may even have influenced your course of action once or twice on the way!

Of course there is more to it all than that. Many people come for readings who are looking for specific information which may be connected to the past, present or future. The sitter may want to know when they can expect to get promoted at work or if they have made a correct decision in some important matter. It is often about their state of health and what spirit recommend as the best course of action. Of course we all have to make our own decisions in life and it is down to free will as to whether we act upon this advice or choose to disregard it.

Never be afraid of those you have loved and lost and never worry that they may be in pain because they had suffered an illness in this life. When we pass on we leave all that behind. Our souls are then healed in the next life and we are purged of all traces of our ailments.

Those that are close to us are given the opportunity of talking to us through sittings without causing us too much distress, which would be greatly amplified if they chose to manifest themselves before our eyes (not to mention the fact that this is difficult for them to do since it requires a large amount of psychic energy). Another way that they may choose to visit us, without distressing us, does not take place at a reading but instead in our dreams.

I would like to elaborate on that last point by using an example. Suppose you were sound asleep one night and found yourself dreaming of your grandfather. He is sitting in his favourite chair in the old house he used to love so much. You enjoyed visiting him there since it was such a warm, happy place and are not surprised to find yourself there again. There you both are, chatting away happily when a third person enters the room and stops. He looks at your grandfather and says "Hey! Why are you here? You're supposed to be dead". Up gets granddad and replies that he is very much alive thank you, and not to be silly. In reality, what has happened here is that your grandfather has chosen to meet with you in an environment that will not disturb or frighten you in any way. You would most probably jump out of your skin if your Granddad were to walk through your front door and sit down for a coffee when you were wide awake and fully aware that he was dead. So, as we all leave our bodies during sleep, spirit often meet with us on the Astral plane, which is best described as the half way point between our two worlds. Here, those wonderful safe surroundings can be created and many happy times can be spent. Sometimes we meet in a beautiful garden which is rife with greenery and light and water flows freely across the land. Even people who cannot remember their dreams will have spent time on the Astral plane with their loved ones. My sister for instance, who would tell you that she has never had a dream about any of the family who have passed on, rang me on one occasion to tell me that for the first time in her life she had dreamt of our grandfather (on my fathers side of the family). This was probably the only dream that Clare has ever remembered and it had a meaning, the relevance of which I will discuss at a later stage in this book.

Paradise

Visions beyond this Earth were shown me
As I in splendid wonder gazed over yonder
To see what I could see

The lush trees and fruit therein
As far as mine eyes could view
The light around me shining bright
It's yellow hues and halo white
And yet no dazzle

Up and beyond were mountains vast
And spring water flowing to the valleys
Rippling; gently flowing by
Passing the gullies into the streams
Bursting with beauty at every seam

My beautiful guide with her ashen white hands
Pointed her finger off to the right
With a wave of her hand I did see revealed
The waters of life spring into sight
They came out of no place to me that I could see

I wanted to cross the revine that did halt
To walk in the gardens and bathe in the stream
But this gaping, vast void had been placed in my path
As it was not yet my time to remain in this place

As I stood in the tunnel I looked up above
The most beautiful colours abounded around
Its purples; Its blues; Its yellows; Its gold
Its pinks and Its creams and Its silver and greens
All cascaded in swirls around us

There then seemed to form a magnificent vale
An old man behind me was saying a prayer
His age was of time long ago and His light was so great
From within Him it flowed
I bowed before Him as I knew Him before
We said our goodbyes but it was sad to go

The darkness engulfed me and I woke into night
But the peace in my heart was still shining through
These wonders were shown for you and for me
I pass on this message and the peace I withdrew
Let those sights and the colours the spirit renew
The peace and the harmony that I wish upon you

****

I hope you now have a clear picture of exactly how we can communicate with spirit. I would now like to share with you several examples of just what kind of information has been brought out in sittings that I have conducted. Each particular example has offered concrete proof to the sitter of life after death and I believe that they will do the same for you, the reader.

When you first start to do a reading for someone you never know what is going to happen, as the first word out of your mouth sets the pace for the reading. This was the case with Pearl. When she first sat down with me I immediately said to her that she had kissed the spirit world. She looked a little startled and replied "Yes I have". I knew that she had been involved in some sort of road accident, as I could see a collision and the force of the impact sending her flying through the air into something solid. I asked if there was a tree nearby this scene and she replied that a tree is what the vehicle had hit. She recalled drifting from her body at that point. I knew there was more to it than this and proceeded on. There appeared to be a strong personality in the room, called William, who was her grandfather. I explained that he was well and happy in spirit and that he was always with her and guiding her. "In fact", I realised, "it was he who had sent you back into your body after the accident as it was not yet your time to go". Pearl was already sure of this and with a tear in her eye told me how she had seen her grandfather during her out of body experience.

I explained to her that the experience she had was a necessary part of her development and that it had, rightly so, changed her life. Pearl had the same gifts as those bestowed upon me, and the time had come for her to take up her spiritual path and start looking deeper within herself. She would be guided forward by a young man, who was related to her family, but who had passed over before she was born. Pearl could relate to this man and was aware of him herself. Towards the end of the reading I gave her some more information about developing her gifts. Pearl is a very enlightened soul spiritually and I feel will go far in her search because of her out of body experience. To me, she has been touched by the spirit world and when this happens your life is never the same again.

My readings are not always conducted for those who have already had concrete experiences, though. Some people, as I have said before, simply come out of curiosity and do not really believe in life after death.

A lady called Rita once visited me through sheer curiosity. As the reading began I told her that her mother and father were with us and that they wanted her to know that a baby was going to be born earlier than it was expected. When I explained this, in awe she said to me, "I doubt that very much. It's a first child". She wouldn't have any of it. I carried on to say that I was being told to tell her that it was a baby boy. Once again, she retorted with a doubting remark. Undaunted, I moved on and asked her if she could place the name Martin since it was an important name to her family. She replied "I don't know anyone called Martin". I persisted with this name and explained that her father was adamant that she accept this name. "I do not know any Martin" was her only response. "Well, it will come out" I said.

The reading continued and I told her how I could see her covered in money and that it had come to her as winnings from something. She laughed out loud and told me not to be so silly as she had never won anything in her life and it was impossible. At this point I stopped the reading and said "I am not taking any of this back. This is what I see and this is what I am giving to you". I then told her not to put all this money into one investment but to use part of it to finance something important to her that she was keen to do, something she dreamt about. Shortly after this the reading came to an end and my sceptical sitter left.

I was to meet Rita again some time later for another reading. I was surprised to find that there was not so much as a peep out of her this time. At the end of the reading she told me about the events that had occurred between her two sittings with me. She described how she had indeed won a large sum of money and decided to do as her mother and father had advised her to do from spirit by splitting her investment. She also told me how shortly after the initial reading she had received a telephone call from her son who was in a hospital with his wife who had just given birth to a baby boy that had been born earlier than expected. She had asked him if he had picked a name for him yet and was told that months earlier they had already decided that the babies name, if a boy, should be Martin! Rita then said "I was reeling from shock from all of this as it all happened so quickly. It must have been within about seven weeks". She then went on to thank me for standing my ground and for putting my trust in what the spirit world was bringing me and also for putting her smile on the other side of her face!

Sometimes, as I have also noted before, people visit me wanting specific information on current events in their lives. These queries are usually connected to personal relationships, both family ties and personal affairs. Steve came to me for a general reading but it soon became apparent that his relatives on the other side wanted him to know that someone very special from the past was about to re-enter his life. I was told to tell Steve that he was very unsure of the relationship he was currently involved in as he still had very strong feelings towards an old girlfriend. I added that this girl, called Ann, was going to come back into his life and that he was literally going to bump into her in the very near future. Steve sat back in the chair as if to say "no way". He told me "I just can't see that happening since I've not seen her for over three years and I haven't the faintest idea where she is. Plus she's married, so it just won't happen". I told him that his Aunt Jenny was asking me to repeat what I had said and that he would see for himself. She was very unhappy too and when they met she would tell him so.

Steve was happy with his reading in general, apart from what I had said about Ann. As he was leaving he turned to me and

said "I'll believe it if it happens and I promise you will be the first to know". With that he left.
I didn't have to wait very long. When I opened the door to my little room the very next day I found a brown envelope on the floor. I picked it up and left it on top of the healing couch that my patients would lie on when receiving treatment. When I got a free moment I sat down and opened the envelope. it was a letter from Steve and it read

> *Dear Tress,*
> *I just had to write this brief note as promised. As I left you yesterday, I had only just gone out of the building when I bumped straight into Ann. I was speechless. I could see that she was very sad and not a bit like the Ann I knew and loved three years ago. We had a long chat and I just wanted to thank you.*
>
> *Steve*

I gathered from his letter that he was not going to let her go so easily this time. On this occasion, spirit were playing Cupid. I personally never under estimate the powers that be and "never say never" - I learned that lesson a very long time ago! A good case to uphold this point is that of Nell.
Nell came to see me for a reading as she had just lost a family member. As it turned out, not only did her father come through (which had been the reason for her visit) but she got quite a surprise too!
I brought through the name Arthur for her and, as she put it, there was not anyone of that name in the family at all and never had been. Nell was sure of this because she had spent considerable time assembling her family tree and had taken it back over a hundred years. Nevertheless I told her to take

it with her as someone in her family may be able to shed more light on it because Arthur was very adamant that he was born into the family. I suggested that there was a Welsh link in her family which might be a good starting point. She was able to confirm this and said that if she found out anything further she would contact me.

Several weeks passed by before the name Arthur was found and it happened in a very unusual way. Nell told me that she had received a 'phone call from a Welsh relative named Caroline, who had told her that there was indeed a family member called Arthur as she had found his birth certificate. It appeared that a family friend, who worked for a local newspaper, had called to Caroline's home. She was in the living room and noticed an old picture hanging on the wall. She felt drawn to it because she was currently writing an article on local history and was in need of old pictures of the area. Since this photo depicted a local site it was ideal. She asked if she could borrow the photo but had said that she would remove it from its frame since the wood was old and delicate and she did not want to damage something so precious. As she removed the back of the frame, an old birth certificate fell from it, belonging to someone called Arthur. This caused great excitement and Nell was immediately informed that I had been indeed correct about this mysterious family member. It had never been noticed before as the picture was never moved, except for dusting and decorating.

I was happy to hear about this since not only was it proof of life after death for Nell and her family, but also because Arthur's appeal to be accepted as part of the family had been acknowledged and confirmed. Thank you Arthur for standing your ground.

The final story that I would like to share with you is a moving account regarding a young lady called Juliet. She had seen me demonstrating my mediumship on several occasions and we had met once or twice, although only very briefly. Early one morning I found a message on my answering machine from this young lady asking if I could call her back as her family were very distressed. She did not say what it was about but she sounded very disturbed so I called her straight away. No sooner had Juliet picked up the receiver at the other end when I saw, revealed to me by spirit, a little girl who stood before me. She told me that there had been an accident and that she had passed over as a result of this. I had just began relaying this to Juliet when I felt such an impact against myself that it nearly flung me across the room. When I caught my breath, I explained to Juliet that I had felt the force of the this tragedy and told her that someone, Heaven knows how, had survived this terrible ordeal. "His name is Jack" I told her, which she confirmed.

I then turned my attention to those members of Juliet's family who had passed on. I could now see a gentleman called George who was wearing a flat cap. "That's true" said Juliet, "he wore one often. He's my mother's father". I knew that George had been sent to rescue the crash victims as they were very confused and did not fully understand what had happened since they had passed so quickly. George was helping them through this.

Following this, I detailed items that had been placed in the victims' coffins, in particular a set of Rosary beads that would not burn during the cremation. "That's right, they were plastic ones" she confirmed. At this point, I decided that it would be best if I saw Juliet and any members of her family who wished to join her for a private reading as there seemed to be special information that the crash victims wanted to pass on to her. A meeting was arranged.

Juliet and her sister-in-law, called Arlene, met me a few days later. It proved to be a very rewarding sitting for all concerned. The flow of energy that came from her family in spirit was very strong considering the force with which they left us. Normally it takes time to build up energy again after a such a turbulent passing. I told Juliet and Arlene that I was seeing a head on collision with some sort of tanker. It was so bad that it seemed that the whole vehicle had been torn apart. As I viewed the crash site, I could see personal belongings, intermixed with wreckage, spread over a great distance. "They never had a chance" I sighed.

I told Juliet that It was being indicated to me by someone with the initial B that this accident did not take place in Leeds. She told me that this must be Bunty, her aunt, who had been killed in the crash. She added that her family had been to see her husband's grandmother who had come over from India, and the accident happened near Northampton. It was Juliet's husband's aunt, cousin Kitty and her little girl Claire who had all been killed in the crash.

The person who had survived the crash, Juliet's uncle Jack, was in a terrible way and was blaming himself for the accident. I told them both that they should keep their eye on him and re-assure him that what happened was not his fault - his family understood that.

Bunty then went on to talk about a ring which seemed to have great sigificance to her and her family. This ring, made of Indian gold, had been in the family for many years and had always been worn by her, yet at the time of her death the ring had not been found. I explained that this ring had been worn in between two others on the third finger of her left hand. Juliet then said that they had had two of the rings returned after the crash but the whereabouts of the third one was still a mystery. They knew it would have been unusual for Bunty to have taken off this ring since it was so special to her. It was at this point that I told them that the ring could still be found at the crash site and they should go back for it. It would be in the grass next to some perfume that had also been missed during the clear up. Juliet and Arlene seemed doubtful about all this since they had been told by police that everything found had been returned and the area had been thoroughly cleared. "Bunty insists that the ring is there" I told them again.

It was several months before Juliet was to make this visit. The family had driven down for the inquest into the accident and decided to stop off at the crash site as they departed Northampton. In the time that had elapsed there had been snow and rain and the grassland where the wreckage had been strewn had grown considerably. Juliet later confessed that her hopes of finding anything further were small. She recalled to me "I suddenly felt a sharp pain in my stomach and heard Arlene shout 'It's here!' ". The ring was found, without a scratch, sitting under some long blades of grass nearby some bottles of perfume; just as Bunty had said.

They called me immediately upon their return home to share the news and their amazement that other details regarding the accident and condition of the bodies had been described in the inquest just as I had described them in my reading. As I do not wish to cause offence to those who have passed or their family, I will not discuss those details, except to say that the reason the ring was separated was because the finger had been severed - just as Bunty had told me months before.

To Juliet and Arlene this was proof of outside influences, independent of both the medium and the sitter, and is positive proof that life exists outside and alongside our world.

11

Stories Of Healing

Since I was a child I have always wanted to heal. I remember as a young girl kissing the Bishop's ring and asking God for this special gift. I have always been very grateful that this wish was granted to me.

Much of the healing I do takes place within my centre in Leeds. I found that I was being asked to do so many healings that it soon became obvious to me that the small room I was using was not going to be sufficient and so I recently moved to the larger premises I now occupy. My new centre has a waiting area and a large main room where patients can sit comfortably and receive healing. As there is much more space to move around I find that much better results are possible. I can walk around them as they lie or sit and access the effected areas of the body much more easily. There have, however, been instances in the past where people were too sick or frail to visit me or I have felt that I have not been in the right location to treat them and so in exceptional circumstances I would go to them. Most of these kind of visits were made to hospitals far and wide. Often I found that the sick would ask relatives to contact me and ask me to visit them in their sick beds.

On one occasion, I was contacted by a young man who asked me if I could call into the local hospital in Leeds as his sister Ann had suffered a stroke and she was very ill indeed. He told me that he had already arranged clearance with the hospital for me to visit her as it was in accordance with her wishes. (I should perhaps tell you at this point that every healer must have not only the permission of the patient but also that of the hospital or care staff. As registered healers, we must abide by certain codes of conduct). I told him that I would be able to see her within the hour and he seemed to be very relieved by this.

I arrived at the hospital as promised and was shown onto the ward by the staff nurse. I introduced myself to Ann and pulled the curtains around the bed so as to afford us some privacy. I could tell she was nervous as she didn't know what to expect and so her brother sat by her bed side to offer reassurance. Ann could not move much at all but was able to tell me that she did still have some feeling in various parts of her body. I spoke gently to her to make her feel more at ease and asked her to relax as much as possible and let the healing flow through her.

I began by giving healing to her arm which had been quite badly affected as she could not lift it at all. I moved my hands up and down the limb letting healing energy pour into it. I did this for several minuets and then withdrew my hands. A few moments passed by and there was nothing, then suddenly Ann's arm started to rise into the air unaided. Ann and her brother looked on in amazement. As her arm moved higher and higher she proclaimed that the feeling was returning through her arm right up to her shoulder.

I was very pleased for Ann and paused for a moment to let her gather herself. I then told her that her uncle had come to give her a message. He wanted her to get out of that bed and go marry her boyfriend as she had kept him waiting long enough!

I then continued my healing and moved towards her legs. I sat on the edge of the bed and gently held my hands over her calves. Once again, as I stepped back, I was able to watch one of her legs raise itself about two feet into the air and then lower itself back down again. As I returned to the bed, I gave the same treatment to her ankles and they too exhibited movement. We all watched them shake and Ann proclaimed at this point that the feeling was returning to her legs too.

The entire session lasted around twenty minutes and upon completion, Ann was a completely different person to the one I had met when I first walked on to the ward. She was laughing and joking and asking all sorts of questions. She was especially curious about how I could have known that she had kept postponing her wedding. I explained that her "special uncle Eddie" had come through and told me.

It was two and a half years later before I had cause to think of this incident again. One of her family had come to see me for a reading and told me in passing that Ann had sent her love and thanks and that she had indeed done as she had been told and got married. She continued "I was also asked to tell you something that you were not told on the day you had visited the hospital. Ann had been given 24 hours to live that day and none of us had expected her to make it through the night. If it had not been for the healing you gave her she may very well have died from the stroke." Ann had been discharged a very short time after my visit and had suffered no further problems since. I must say I was overjoyed to hear this news as it is so nice to get feedback from healings. So often you never hear from these people again or only when they have another condition that they want help with. Sometimes the only way I get to learn is when someone visits me who has heard about my work through recommendation.

Whatever the reason, it is always wonderful to hear just how much benefit some people can get through healing.
Another similar case involved a gentleman called John. A member of John's family had heard about me and asked if I could help him as the doctors had said it was only a matter of time now and there was very little that they could still do for him. He was in a great deal of pain from a terrible cancer and he himself was ready to give up hope. When I heard about this I impressed upon her that at this late stage I could not guarantee miracles but would do whatever I could to help. I arranged to visit John that evening.
John's bed was downstairs in the front room as he was in so much pain that he could not sit up, let alone walk up a flight of stairs. I sat chatting with him for a while as spiritual healing was foreign to him and he had no idea what it entailed or even if he should believe in it, since he had severe doubts about life after death. I soon had him questioning that doubt as I was able to bring many members of his family through who recounted many wonderful times with him and it wasn't long before John was engaged in fits of laughter at those happy memories. There were so many people from spirit gathered round the bed with him that it was difficult to keep track of who was called what and who was standing where!
As soon as I could see that John was at ease I gently put my hands on his chest and allowed spiritual healing to flow through them into his body. Within moments he was telling me that the pain was subsiding and that he was finding it easier to breathe, the cancer had spread quickly throughout his whole body and I asked spirit to show me the effected areas so that I might channel energy into them too.
I spent over an hour with John that night and promised to return the following evening to continue the treatment. We

had become like old friends in only an evening and I was thrilled to see him so at ease and comfortable.

My visits to John were quite numerous and regular and he would look forward to each and every one of them. If I was even five minutes late for an appointment he would become anxious. His belief and trust were important to both myself and his family as it gave them the courage to accept John's condition but take heart in the fact that he was being able to live out his time (and probably a much longer period of time at that) in comfort and happiness.

John's sense of humour came thundering back to him as the pain diminished and he was even able to get out of bed and walk a little or simply sit by the fire as his circulation was very poor. I would sit here with John and talk about the spirit world and what it was like over there and answer any questions that he had. He would ask things like "Will the cancer disappear when I cross over?" and "When will I go and will I be able to come back and see my family?" I told John that he would feel as light as a feather when he passed, and over a period of time he would feel like the John he used to be, since the cancer would have left him. He would retain everything he had experienced in this life in his spirit body and would be free to visit his family if he so wished. He seemed to take all this in and was happy with the knowledge that there is indeed life after death and that it just doesn't stop when we pass.

The last time I was with John I gently put my hands on his chest and gave him healing. His breathing had deteriorated quite rapidly and I found that the best thing I could do for him now was just to sit on the edge of his bed and hold his hand. My guide told me that my part in this was over now. I said goodnight to John and I knew I would never see him like this again. Two days later I received a call to say that

John had died. He had told his family who were congregated around his bedside at the time that he could see nuns nearby and that he felt peace and was not afraid to die. With that he was gone.

On the Sunday after John had passed on I was standing by the washing machine and I felt a hand on the back of my head stroking my hair. When I turned around to see who it was there was nobody there. I then heard a voice say "There, I told you she would feel it". I could then see John clairvoyantly, looking radiant and happy. I saw him again that same night. I awoke from my sleep to see him standing beside the bed, handing me a red rose. We call these spiritual rose's because they never die. This was John's way of thanking me for being there in his hour of need. I thanked him for letting me know he was okay and promised that I would share the news with his family.

I called his family the day after to give them the news, and at the same time arranged a consultation with them to offer counselling. Needless to say, John came through straight away at the meeting and brought with him an abundance of evidence to prove that there is life after death. One member of the family decided to perform a test to make sure if it really was John. They asked him "Were the dishes that you once brought home worth anything?" to which he replied, "Stop being so nosy. I wouldn't tell you then and I'm not going to tell you now". I saw him raise his finger to his nose and smile cheekily. His family confirmed that this was his usual response to this question and this left no doubt in their minds that this really was John.

John's mother Betty came to see me for healing as she had a lung condition and John would come with her. As I tried to help from this side, John was on the other side of the vale doing his bit for her too.

John has a wonderful sense of humour. He will often remind me of the rose he gave by appearing in fancy dress with a rose clenched in his teeth. Betty had told me that he once dressed up like this in fancy dress. It is John's way of getting his mother to laugh when she was feeling down. I really do believe that part of the reason I was brought to meet John is so that I would be there for his mother after his passing as she missed him terribly.
Unfortunately, Betty let go of her life on this plain on the 19th of November 1995. She is now reunited with her beloved son. So peace, love and light to you both. God Bless.

****

As I have mentioned earlier, people will often come to me for healing after having spoken to someone who has been to see me in the past with an ailment or illness. Lesley, who lived in Spain, was one such lady.
She heard of me through a family member who was being treated by me. She was responding well to the process and was improving every day. Thus it appeared that Lesley decided to make the journey from Spain to see me, hoping that I could do something for her.
Lesley had been a victim of a car crash which had left her quite badly injured. She was constantly in and out of hospital for treatment and had undergone several major operations on her arm which was severely scarred due to the accident and operations. She had hardly any use of this arm and would find it difficult even to lift a cup. It seemed there was a problem with her elbow that none of her eight operations could fix. I told her I would do what I could.
I began to give her healing and followed the instructions of the other side as to how I should progress. I was working my

way down her arm as directed when I felt that I should take hold of her hand in mine. Her right hand was partly unusable since two of her fingers were bent and unmoveable. As I did this she looked a little surprised and told me "You will never straighten my fingers. The specialist told me that the nerves there have been severed". I ignored her comments and proceeded anyway.

I spent around twenty minutes administering healing and after I had finished I asked if she could feel any benefit from it. She tried to move her arm and said that it felt much easier to move than it had done for a long time. With that I suggested we meet again and administer some more healing as I knew that more could be done for her.

Two days later, Lesley returned with her sister for her second appointment and I asked her how she was feeling. This time she seemed more optimistic and told me that she had even more movement and was feeling a lot less pain than she was accustomed to. Pleased that there had been progress, I began another round of healing. I recall that I had forgotten that she had no feeling in her fingers but remember that my grandfather had instructed me to take her hand in mine again as before. And so I put my thumb inside the palm of her hand, just under her last two fingers which were those that were bent. I gently began to rub the palm of her hand and then I was told by spirit to clasp her hand in between my own. In order to do this I had to put each of my hands just above her wrist so that her fingers were all straight in between my hands. I then slid my hands down towards her fingertips. "All done now" I said in a soft voice.

I stood back to ask how she was feeling. At first, neither her or her sister spoke, preferring instead to look at each other with some kind of bewilderment. They then both started crying. I waited for a time for them to stop, not fully understanding what it was that I had missed and eventually asked why they were both so emotional. "Don't you remember?" asked Lesley. I must have looked a little puzzled since she then continued. "Two days ago I could not straighten my hand yet now it is straight and I can move my fingers as if nothing has happened!" I believe that spirit healed her hand as if to say "Never say never !"

About six weeks later I heard that a piece of bone had worked it's way out of her arm through the skin and Lesley's ability to use her arm has increased dramatically and over two years later, her arm and hand are doing fine.

Denise, who is Lesley's sister and was with her at the time of her miraculous healing, has also had treatment from me. Denise suffers from ME (similar to MS) and on her initial visits to see me she was suffering very badly from it. It would take her hours in the morning to begin to feel anything close to normal and she was having to take a lot of time off work to rest. Since Denise is a nurse, who need to be dependable, this was causing problems and she was at her wits end. Hence, after my work with her sister, she asked if myself and spirit could do anything to help her.

Her condition is one which affects the muscles and nervous system and causes prolonged periods of pain and discomfort. On our first session, I helped her up onto my healing couch and placed my hands at the tips of her feet and worked my way up her whole body since all areas tend to be affected. The healing lasted around twenty minutes, which is a fairly standard time.

I asked her how she was feeling, to which she replied "Marvellous compared to how I felt when I came in". She said her body was tingling from head to toe. I explained that this was merely the healing energy continuing to do it's work within the body and it was nothing to worry about.

As the effect of the healing became more apparent to her she said she hadn't felt this good in years and started crying. The pain and listlessness seemed to have been totally removed from her. I was very happy for her and glad that spirit had been able to help her so much.

Denise made several more visits over the ensuing months and eventually found that she was able to live a totally different life. She was able to walk unassisted for long periods of time and also found that she could drive a car without any difficulty. Not so long ago she joined her sister in Spain, but still pops in to say "Hello" when she's back in the country to visit her mother. Their mother thinks it is unbelievable that healing has changed the lives of both her daughters. I'm just happy to have played a part.

There are many such cases of healing that I could put forward for your consideration. One such story involved a reading for a lady called Jane, in which I was able to bring her father through who had passed on some years earlier. I felt the need from him to ask her about a back and lung condition that someone within her family was suffering from and sensed that her father wanted me to give some healing on these affected areas.

She left feeling very uplifted and a short while later called me to make a healing appointment for her husband who suffered badly with emphysema. An appointment was arranged for them to come and see me at my Centre. Her husband, Alan, was in a wheelchair at the time since he'd had his leg amputated shortly before our meeting. He was happy for me to give some gentle healing on his lungs and chest although he seemed a little sceptical since he had never encountered anything like it before. I fixed another appointment with them for the following week and so it went on.

About a month later Alan told me that his chest was feeling much better, so much so that at his regular hospital check up the doctors thought that he had stopped smoking! He told them he was seeing a spiritual healer. He then asked me would I help him by healing his 'good' leg since the specialists had told him that they would have to amputate it as the circulation was so bad. His leg was turning black. I did not promise anything but said I would do what I could.

After several healing sessions, Alan had to go back to the hospital for another examination by the specialists. This time he was told that there had been a vast improvement in the condition of his leg and the blood flow was much better. They told him that they would monitor the situation and that if it continued to improve there would be no need to amputate.

On the last occasion I had need to give Alan healing I recall being instructed to move my hands to the ball of his foot. I poised it there for a moment as I was almost in a trance state. Suddenly I heard my grandfather shout "That's it" and I came around. I felt certain that Alan would not need to visit me again.

After his next hospital visit, I was very pleased to hear that he had been told by the specialist that they had found a pulse in his leg - for the first time in two years! He was given the all clear and told not to come back. Obviously Alan and his wife were thrilled and called to share the good news with me. Thank you spirit for allowing Alan to keep his leg.

****

Sometimes, people would approach me for healing when I was out in public at services and demonstrations. There are two accounts of this in particular that I would like to share

with you.
The first example took place when I was doing an evening of clairvoyance in Wetherby one Saturday night. I had reached the point in the evening where I was discussing healing and about how it is possible to identify ailments from the breakdown in the aura. I was looking around the room at the various aura's of those in attendance when I was drawn to a lady who was sat about four rows back and slightly off to the side. I could see in her aura that she had problems with both of her ankles, probably the result of some accident she had suffered. I told her about this and advised her to be especially careful of the right ankle as it was very weak and needed strapping up. She was very insistent that I was wrong and it was the left ankle that was in need of attention, not the right one. As usual, I stood my ground and repeated what I had said. I then asked her if she had been in an accident, which she was able to confirm. I then spoke a little about her husband in spirit who was sending his love and left it at that.
About a week later I got a 'phone call. The lady on the other end gave me her name, Pat, and said I would remember her since she was the one who had insisted I had picked the wrong ankle at my special evening in Wetherby. I did, of course, remember and asked how I could help her, to which she replied, "I have got something to tell you. I was rehearsing on the stage two days ago when I moved too close to the turn table on the stage. I turned to avoid it and heard my right ankle go 'click' below me. Next thing I knew I had fallen over. My leg is now in plaster!" She went on "I wish I had listened to you because now I won't be able to appear in the stage production at the end of the month. All my hard work has been for nothing." I could see clairvoyantly that healing needed to take place and so I told her I would meet

her to see what I could do for her. I was certain that the plaster could be off in a week and I told her this over the 'phone. I then gave her an appointment and met her shortly after.

I gave Pat healing by positioning my hand over the affected area and, as was standard, the session lasted about twenty minutes. "There", I said "You will be in your production as scheduled". Pat was highly sceptical about this but then seemed to think better of it since I had been right about the ankle. "I do hope so" she replied.

Pat did indeed have the plaster off her leg within the week and appeared in the Opera as planned. As a way of thanks she presented me with two tickets and I sat and watched as she gave a glowing performance.

I see and hear from Pat from time to time and will often smile at her scepticism. Pat no longer doubts that there is something more to life than that which we can see and is now what I would call a 'true believer'.

The second story of healing that I would like to share with you involves a wonderful little lady called Laura. In 1992, Laura became very ill with acute myloide leukaemia, which is a very severe form of the illness. Her frail body was subjected to months of intense chemotherapy in a bid to combat the problem but the results left her extremely weak and damaged her heart.

At the time Laura's predicament was brought to my attention, a search had been instigated to find a suitable donor for a bone marrow transplant that she was in desperate need of. Laura's sister, Michelle, was found to be compatible but at that point the operation was deemed too risky since Laura was so ill. It was Laura's aunt that first told me of all this, when she visited me for a reading. She asked me for advice about her niece and I advised her to go ahead with the transplant.

Partly because of this advice, a second opinion was sought from doctors as to the severity of Laura's heart condition. It was diagnosed that it was not as bad as had been previously thought, and so the operation took place in August 1992.

Although it was a success, by November a number of complications had arisen. Laura went down with pneumonia for the second time that year and then developed liver failure. She was growing worse every day. It was at this time that I was to become much more involved with Laura and her family.

Laura's mother, Christine, decided to visit me herself. Initially, I was unaware of who she was as nothing had been said upon the making of the appointment, but it did not take long for me to get to the crux of the matter. Christine recalled to me recently "As soon as you asked 'What happened four months ago to cause you such distress?' I knew you were on the right track. It was four months ago that very day when I was in St. James' Hospital, very upset because Laura was being given oxygen for pneumonia. Then I had received a phone call saying that my son Michael had fallen down and fractured his skull!" During this time, poor Christine was having to go from one side of the hospital to the other to see her two children who were placed in different wards.

I knew that I had to see Laura for myself as I needed to give her some healing. "I couldn't bring Laura to see you" Christine continued, "since she was virtually housebound and in isolation because we didn't want her picking up any more infections. Thankfully, you came along to the house the very next night."

When I saw Laura that first time, I was amazed to see just how full of life and sparkling she still was, despite her severe afflictions. She is a remarkably clever little girl and is very strong willed and determined. I was not at all surprised that she responded so well to the spiritual healing she received and I kept going to see her, sometimes up to three nights a week, for healing. By May, Laura was in remission and back at school.

"I used to work as a waitress in a restaurant" said Christine "and when people heard about Laura they started fund-raising for her. She had become so much better. It wasn't long before we had collected enough for us to treat her to a holiday so we took her to Disneyland, which she loved."

The time I spent with Laura was very dear to me. There were some tense moments when things were looking very bad for her but Laura and her family had faith in spirit and I hope that I was able to help them through all those difficult times. Thank you spirit for giving Laura another chance.

A Child

A child born of this world holds no malice
A child of this world knows no fear
A child born of this world has complete trust
A child born of this world cries only for its simple needs
A child asks for nothing else; it demands nothing else
A child's young life is simplicity itself

But as a child grows it sees the ways of Mankind
A child learns from what it accrues first of all from its own surroundings
A child listens with intent: to learn, delve and discover
Its tiny mind takes in every detail, the personality of its surroundings
The child learns from this and grows and flows

For it sees the signs - every touch; every smile; every tone; every frown
The subconscious forms the basis for the child's strength and weakness
For its growth and compassion
You could call it the invisible tree of life
We can strengthen its branches, or we can stunt its growth

I hope there are many more children brought into this world Laura, who are as special as you.

****

A final little anecdote on healing for you. It is not only to adults and children that I have given healing, but animals too! I recall a recent visit to a friend who owned a Yorkshire Terrier. When I walked through the door I saw that she was carrying the little mite in her arms and it did not look very well at all. I knew immediately that it had been poisoned. I asked if I could hold him a while but the girl was doubtful if he would allow it because he didn't like to be held, especially by strangers. "He'll be fine" I told her. And so I took him in my arms. He was as good as gold! I stroked his tummy until I clairvoyantly heard a man's voice tell me that my job was done. With that, I gave him a little cuddle and then passed him back to his owner.
Within an hour, the wee chap had perked up and ate a little food. The girl decided to take him to the vet to make sure he was okay and so I left. It was a couple of weeks later when I next heard from her. She told me that he had indeed been poisoned and the vet had been amazed that he had survived. I just smiled and said a silent prayer of thanks to spirit. He lived to lift his leg another day!

Bertie the cat, the beginning of The Psychic Pet Detective!

My husband, Joe.

Laura, who is a big girl now, seen here at the time of her illness, aged 5.

My father, Jack (top right) and uncle Dan (top left). Sitting in front on the right is my brother Joseph.

My mother, Teresa Hayden, pictured here in her early thirties.

The only photograph of my beloved grandmother, who watches over me.

Myself and Tulsa, enjoying the rare British sunshine.

12

Premonitions And Dreams

As I've already outlined earlier in this book, there are many ways in which spirit can communicate with us and show things to us that have not yet happened. The ability to decipher both dreams and premonitions has run strong in my family for generations and I remember discussing the experiences that my mother had on several occasions.

I recall how she once told me about the incident that first caused her to think that there may be more to this life than meets the eye. It happened when my mother was just a young girl, still living at home in Kilbeggan with the family. One evening, two of her cousins had been to visit. the time had grown quite late and so her cousins said their farewells and left, leaving my granddad to lock up the house for the night and the family retired for a nights' rest. At about two o'clock in the morning, there was a loud banging at the front door and granddad went down to answer it. There stood the two cousins, white with fright. They pushed their way inside and told granddad how they'd been travelling the dark roads home when they'd come across a stranger on a horse, stationary in the middle of the road. They had paused to greet this person and enquire as to who he was - but he vanished from sight before their very eyes. They turned their own horses around and raced straight back to the house.

My mother had many, more personal, spiritual experiences in her life but was always very unsure of using her gift, possibly because she didn't understand it fully. It may have also been because it frightened her a little. She had once foreseen the death of a friends child which proved extremely distressing for her, especially as she chose not to tell her friend about it. This is called a premonition, or a vision of something from the future that has yet to happen. After this experience, she refused to use her gift again

I think I learned a lot from my mother regardless of the fact that she chose to shut off her own abilities. When things did come to me, I like to think I was a little more aware of what was happening and not quite as afraid. I also believe that my mother may have been meant to close her gift off, whereas I was not, which is why I was still constantly plagued by experiences even though I too, for a time, had chosen to shut it out.

My own premonitions started when I was very young. As I've said before, I had a tremendous affection for the old people in the area I grew up in and I remember one very special lady, called Kitty. Kitty used to buy some of the firewood I would sell after school. She was not a well woman, as she suffered with chronic arthritis, and only managed to survive thanks to the help of her loving niece and the few neighbours who would pop around and do odd jobs for her. I used to sit with Kitty and keep her company, as she was practically bed ridden. I would light a fire for her and bring her cups of tea and sometimes rub ointment on her back to stop bed sores from forming. She was very outspoken, which back then was something that a woman was not meant to be! She either liked you immediately or would not tolerate you - there was no in between. Fortunately, she and I got on very well.

One Saturday morning, I called in to see Kitty but her door hadn't been unlocked. Her door was padlocked from the outside so that those with keys were the only ones who could gain access. Since Kitty could not get out of bed, this had never been a problem. Normally, her next door neighbour would have been in at this point to give Kitty her breakfast, but it seemed she had been running a little late that day and was only just finishing her breakfast. She asked me to take her key and go prop Kitty up in bed ready for her meal.

I unlocked the door and put my head around it to say good morning. Kitty, however, was nowhere to be seen. The covers on the bed were pushed right back. My first thought was that she must have fallen out of bed and so I ran to the far side of the room to check. She wasn't there. I checked the back room but there was still no sign. I did not understand this since Kitty had no way of getting out of bed by herself, let alone leaving the flat since she had no key and the door, as I said, was locked from the outside.

I ran back across the landing and told the neighbour that Kitty wasn't there. Naturally, as I was but a mere child and she was a wise old adult, she believed none of it and insisted I was wrong. Nevertheless I insisted what I had said was true and so the neighbour picked up the breakfast tray and walked across to Kitty's flat. I followed her inside, amazed to find Kitty back in bed and alive and well. I did not know what to think.

I played the scene out in my mind several times over the next few months, and remained convinced that Kitty had indeed disappeared. Then one day as I went to see her, as I had done many times in the past, I walked in to find the room empty and bedclothes pulled right back just as they had been before. I then learned that Kitty had been rushed

to hospital and had since passed on.
It appears that I witnessed Kitty's passing several months beforehand and had not realised it. This was my first real experience of premonition.
I have seen many events transpire that I have had prior knowledge of. Some have gone on to become National (and International) news. Does it upset me? I would have to say at the time that it does, because most of the predictions I am given concern misfortune or suffering. It is sad that this is the case but what I see is beyond my control. I always try to remember that I have a gift and not question why one event should be shown to me as opposed to another.
There is an instance I can think of when I was giving a reading to a young lady. She had never been to see me before and I think the whole experience was something quite new to her. I began the reading by bringing through a number of relatives, friends and loved ones who had passed on and gradually went on to more general information. I recall asking her if she had an American relative. She replied "No" to this but I wasn't happy to leave it there. I requested that she check with her family because they would know. I then explained why this was so important.
I could see a plane that was carrying the relative I had just spoken of on it. I knew that it was definitely tied in with America because I could see J.F.K. airport. I told her that I was watching an explosion on the plane and glass, metal and smoke were being strewn everywhere. People were falling all over the place, not knowing what was happening to them.
Some time later I got a phone call from her asking if a relative from The States could come to see me. Since the nature of the visit was so sensitive, I agreed that I would see them that evening at my home. It appeared that the young girl had forgotten to follow up on my request to search out

her American relative. Sadly, my prediction had been correct and an American family member had been killed in the Lockerbie aeroplane disaster of 1988.

Through this appalling and senseless event, a mother came to claim her son's body and wanted to see the lady who saw this precognition in the hope that I could let her know if her son was at peace. Her son came through and let her know that he was with his grandparents in spirit, and told her that he was recovering from the shock of being thrown into the spirit realm so suddenly. This offered some comfort to the poor woman but it was such an unnecessary tragedy.

People can often ask why I, and others like me, do not alert the authorities of such disasters and prevent them from happening. Unfortunately, very little notice is taken of those who do try to and the ways of man will have to undergo rigorous change before that fact alters. I do what I can for who I can, but I cannot influence the free will of others to make their own choices. If they disbelieve what is told to them - that is up to them.

Sometimes, though, the information given by spirit is much more vague and cryptic. I remember being on a coach travelling back to Leeds from Dublin, where Joe and I had spent four days demonstrating my mediumship and lecturing. We had worked very hard, sometimes well into the small hours, but the people there were very kind and it was a wonderful challenge. I had begun dozing on the coach and no sooner had I shut my eyes when a vision of sorts was brought before me. I was firstly shown men playing bagpipes, and so I assumed that whatever was going to happen would take place in Scotland. Curious, I watched a little longer. Then appeared before me a scene where metal had become so hot that it was twisting and snapping. I could see smoke bellowing out all around and there were faint cries of panic in the distance. I sat up with a start saying "Oh my God, those poor men". Joe looked at me and asked what was wrong. I explained to him what I had seen and that there was going to be some sort of disaster in Scotland, although I couldn't tell exactly what it would be. I could not explain though, the relevance of the pipers I had seen.

I was to discover in the news shortly afterwards that there had indeed been a disaster in Scotland. It was Joe who put the paper down in front of me. The headline read something like 'Piper Alpha Rig Destroyed'. The vision then made sense since I could then tell that the bagpipe players were meant to signify Piper; and everything else shown had been the destruction of the rig. I do not believe that there was anything I could have done about this, since the clues were vague and no indication of the time of the catastrophe had been given by spirit. I would like to give hope though to the families of those who lost their lives on the rig by saying that they are at peace now and with loved ones who had gone on before them. They have just gone before you to prepare a place for you and you will be together again one day. Not all visions are this grim though.

Another time Joe and I were on a coach on our way to sail to Dublin, I was given a vision of some children who were being taken hostage by a man, they too were on a coach or a bus.

I felt very calm on this occasion although some of the children appeared to be distressed, but some others on the coach kept their heads and this helped the other children. The scene then changed to a happy one. I could see the children smiling and they were getting off the coach safe and sound and all was well.

I turned to Joe and told him of what I had seen and said this one has a happy ending.

We were sitting in my sister-in-laws lounge a couple of days later when the news came on and Joe happened to overhear the newsreader say "A coach was hijacked in Belfast today. Several children were on board but all were released safe and well" And so you can see that visions can sometimes prove beneficial. What is more, they can even be lifesavers for the person who is having them.
I was on stage one Friday night, talking to my husband in a night-club he had worked at for many years. He was setting up his equipment as he was about to start work. I had taken him up an orange drink since once he started working, he didn't like to be disturbed. Friday night was the time I would go out with Joe and get together with all our friends. Normally, it was a very good night, but this particular time I did not feel my usual, jolly self. Instead I was withdrawn and I could feel my insides turning. My friends began to notice as the night progressed since I was not participating in the conversation much. when they asked what was wrong, I would simply say that it had been a long day and I was tired. I did not want to tell them about the dread I was feeling inside, since that night I had a terrible vision - about myself. I never told my friends about my gift, since I didn't like using it and didn't know how they would react. If ever I had a message come through for them I would simply give it out as advice and not identify its true source. Since this was the case, I could not tell them what I was seeing that night. I knew I had to tell someone and so I went to tell Joe.
I told him that I would have a serious health problem, not now, but when I was about forty-two. I would be given a warning closer to the time and if I did not take heed of it then I would be dead within months. If I did choose to act on it, though, there would be a tremendous change in my life and a whole new responsibility would be mine. Joe

looked blankly at me when I told him all this as it certainly came out of the blue. I gave him a moment to gather his thoughts and start the next record. "Don't be talking like that" he said. He could tell that I was serious. "It will happen" I told him. With that, I immediately felt as if a great weight had been lifted from my shoulders and I went back down to my friends and enjoyed the rest of the night.

Just as my forty-second year was approaching, I became very ill. I lost over two and a half stone in weight. I am five foot five inches in height so I must have looked quite awful.

I decided to go for a check up since one was long overdue but I've never liked going to the doctors. When I saw her I told her that I had two problems but the doctor doubted this, insisting that there was possibly only on thing wrong which we would learn from the tests I had done.

Four days later, the surgery called to say that they had made an appointment for me at St. James' Hospital to see a specialist and I would receive confirmation in the post. It seemed that some abnormal or pre-cancerous cells had shown up on the tests and they wanted to check me over again and decide on a course of action. It was at this time that I began to think back to what I had told Joe all those years before.

When I told Joe about this he remembered my prediction vividly; the night; the time; the place. He could even recall the records that were in the charts, like "Shooting Star" by Dollar.

When I went to St. James', they told me I would need an operation to have these cells removed. It was to be some kind of laser treatment which would burn away the infected tissues. This was a very simple, routine operation and I would only be an out-patient. This was what they first thought. They then did a biopsy and found that the cells were much more advanced than had previously been thought and so I would have to be admitted and go under general anaesthetic.

Before my operation, I was told by spirit that I would bring back strong proof of life after death for those around me. I was quite curious as to what they were going to do since I would be completely out of it with the anaesthetic! Sure enough though, when I had been administered with the anaesthetic, my guide came forth and told me that the nurse and the porter who would take me to the ER would not be the same people who would be standing beside me when I came to. She then told me to relax and watch what was going to happen.

I then found I was looking at myself sat on a stool, surrounded by a circle of spirit people. The circle rose up in tiers and closed in on itself towards the top. The concentration of energy up there was enormous and bright light shone down on me. No words were spoken and yet I could clearly hear these beings talking to me. I was told that I had to bring back a message. When I opened my eyes, there would be a lady standing to my right and a man on the left. The message, which they proceeded to give to me, was for the lady. I then heard my guide say that it was time for me to go back. I did not want to go though, because it was serene and peaceful there, but it seemed I had no choice.

When I opened my eyes, there was indeed a woman to my right and gentleman to the left. I told the lady that I had been speaking to her nanny who wanted her to know that the baby girl she had been praying for was on the way. She also wanted her to know that her husband would be spending a lot of time in the future working in London. I then told her that she was missing her nanna but there was no need, because she was right here. By now, the lady was crying and told me that it was all true and that she believed in what I did and what I said as she had been to a spiritual church before. With that, I was wheeled back to the ward by herself and the gentleman, who was a doctor. As they pushed me along, they told me that they had found it very difficult to bring me round and that I had been unconscious much longer than was usual. They had grown quite concerned at one point as my breathing had become so shallow and had given me oxygen.

When we were alone on the ward, she told me she had been praying for a baby girl for a long time. She already had a son. She then asked if one of the other nurses could sit with me for a while since she had recently been bereaved. I had come back to my senses very quickly so I agreed. I think I had read for half the staff by the time I left!

Unfortunately for me though, my health problem did not go away as easily as the doctors had anticipated. The second problem I had foreseen then came to light. I began suffering with a great deal of pain and discomfort and despite many courses of tablets and various treatments, it was decided that I would have to undergo a partial hysterectomy.

The second time I found myself in hospital in connection with the above I underwent a similar experience although this time I was given no warning by spirit that I would be bringing anything back with me.

Once I was put under the anaesthetic I found myself back in that same place. I now call it the Hall Of Knowledge. Before me was a very beautiful lady who wanted to express her concern about the well being of a young lady that I would meet when I came around after my operation. She gave her name as Margaret and told me she was a relative of the lady in question. As I watched her, she took out a pack of tarot cards and spread them out at my feet. She pointed to them one by one, and asked me if I knew what they meant. I told her that I did and that I would remember their meaning to pass on. With that, she smiled and told me the lady I must speak to was called Carol.

As I opened my eyes after the operation, I was already calling out to Carol. She was a trainee anaesthesiologist, I later learned, and she was stood in the theater trying to bring me around. I told her that I had been talking to Margaret who had informed me that "you have had a very bad tarot reading. She wants you to know that you have not to take any notice of it at all because it was all untrue". I knew she had been told to give up her studies and that she should not marry her fiancee as he was the wrong person. "Do not give up your studies because you have found your vocation and stay with your partner because he is a good man and the right one for you". By now the girl was in tears with relief. "Margaret has reached out to you from spirit to put this wrong right."

I spoke to Carol later when she was off duty and she told me how she had felt like taking an overdose after her tarot reading. She thought that she had wasted her life. She said that whilst I was still unconscious I had been talking, telling her that I was speaking with her gran and I would be with her soon. She just could not believe that I knew her first name and had come back with such wonderful information. She was very grateful to both me and her gran for restoring her faith in her work and for putting her life right again. If my operations were simply to help these people then they were worthwhile.

It is difficult to categorise whether my experiences in hospital were premonitions or dreams. I suppose that they were an element of both. Some cases, however, are a little more clear cut. Like a story regarding my uncle Dan.

As I have said before, I was always very fond of Dan, even

though I never got to see him very often because he lived so far away. He was very much into family and believed in keeping in touch and would visit mum whenever he could as they were very close. I would often send good wishes to him in my mother's letters and I know that when she moved back to Ireland in 1980 she was very pleased to have the opportunity to spend more time with him. Dan had to visit a specialist in Dublin every few weeks due to illness and so it gave him an opportunity to see mum regularly.

One September night in 1987 I dreamt about Dan. In my dream I was back in Dublin standing in front of a row of shops that I knew well. There was someone stood with me, but I couldn't tell who it was. There was a funeral procession taking place. As I looked ahead, I could see my mother sat in a car with three other people that I didn't recognise. They appeared to be following the procession behind lots of other people and I remember getting an impression that quite a few of them were Scottish, although I don't recall exactly how I knew that. The crowd was sombrely walking down past Saint Teresas Gardens, which is where I grew up, towards St Teresas Church. I could then see that it was Dan standing beside me, smiling. He was standing with one of his sisters. "Don't forget to tell your mother I brought Nancy with me" he said. I knew that uncle Dan had passed away.

The next morning I wrote a letter to mum telling her what I had seen. I told her Dan had passed on and of the message he had given. I also asked her who the Scottish relatives were in the procession. I knew that the letter would take about three days to reach her but she had no 'phone so I could not call her.

Only two days after, I received a letter from her saying that Dan had passed. He had come in from work (he was in his mid-sixties) and told his wife that he was tired and going for

a lie down on the settee for a while. His wife had gone to cover him as she thought he looked very pale, and then realised that he had passed quietly, in his sleep.
I then had a further letter from mum telling me that just two weeks before his passing he had been to see her and they had had a very strange conversation. He had asked her if she thought there was anything more than this (life) to which mum replied "I hope so. There must be something better to go to than this world." He had then made a promise that if he died before her and there was life after death, he would find a way of telling her and that he would bring Nancy with him. My mum thought it was odd that he would talk about dying, since he was several years younger than her. But perhaps he had seen his own passing?
There were Scottish relatives at the funeral. I suppose this was Dan's way of showing that no family ties should ever be severed. I'm pleased he found a way to keep his promise to my mother.

****

On Earth, we are separated by borders, continents and water but there are no such borders in the spirit world. One night in 1993 whilst I was asleep I had the great pleasure of meeting someone who I would never possibly have met in the conscious world.
I remember being aware that I was asleep yet I knew that I was not dreaming. I was alone in a big bright room, sitting in a hardback chair with a list of some kind in my hand. I couldn't make sense of it at all. I felt a little strange because I could feel I was being watched. This sensation grew stronger as did the light in the room. I could see mists swirling around me and another figure walk out from it in

front of me. I recognised the man. He had brought joy to millions through his acting and singing and was a world class entertainer. He was wearing a well made grey suit and looked in his early forties.

He walked up to me and asked if his name was on the list. His name was there but it was clearly not yet his time to pass as it was way down near the bottom. "you can't go through yet" I told him "you have a little time left and some unfinished business to take care of." I told him that he needed medical help as his liver and stomach were well past their best. He smiled that charismatic smile of his that many of us have come to know so well over the years. It was Dean Martin. Then he was gone.

The next morning, I told Joe about it all. I always tell him when something strange happens so that he can keep his eye on the media and corroborate what I say.

Over the next week, there seemed to be something of a Dean Martin extravaganza. His records were never off the radio and several of his films were shown on television. Then came the news in a national newspaper that he had checked himself into a clinic for tests.

A few weeks later, there was another article in the papers saying that Dean Martin only had four months to live and that he was riddled with cancer. His liver was shot from years of the high life, but he was the first to say that he had no regrets. "I'm just looking forward to heaven" he said. A photo of him in a grey suit accompanied the article.

I have often wondered if Dean Martin had the same vision that night, because I do truly believe that he was there with me. At the time of writing this, he is alive and well. *

* Dean Martin passed away on Christmas Day 1995, two years after my experience. He was a very special man and I wish him well in his onward journey.

13

Using My Gift In Other Ways

I have been asked many times if I ever use my gift to win money. I can categorically say that I do not. My gift is not meant to be used in this way. However, spirit have shown me in the past that it is possible.

I recall a time that I had stayed overnight at my sister-in-law's house. It was about 1981. I remember having a dream about a race that was going to take place and being told by spirit to take special notice of the colours of the horses. I felt strangely drawn to the darkest coloured horse that was running and, as I watched, the horse took the lead and went on to win the race. I felt I had been shown all this because I was meant to put a bet on this race, even though I did not have the name of the horse.

The next day when I awoke and went downstairs for breakfast, I asked to see the morning paper. My husband Joe handed me the paper that his father, Maurice, had just brought back from the shops. I then told everyone about my dream and looked at the horses running that day. With the help of my father-in-law, I was able to identify the darkest coloured horse that was running and I asked Maurice if he would place a bet of a few pence for me since it was going to win. He decided to gamble on my dream too, as the horse was an outsider and any winnings would amount to quite a sizeable amount.

I won about twelve pounds that day, so we all enjoyed having a good meal on the winnings. I never asked Maurice how much he had won, but he did have a nice smile on his face for the rest of the day!

Several years later, I made acquaintance with a lady called Meg who owned a part share in a race horse which I shall call King Pin. I got to telling Meg about my little windfall one day and she began asking me questions about her own horse. Meg wanted to place a bet on the next race that her horse understood and wanted to know if it would win. "No", I replied, "but it will come in placed". I did not see the harm in telling her that much since it would only amount to a very small amount of winnings for her, anyway.

Meg often made other requests for information about her horse but I proved more candid in what I would tell her. Then one day I received a very strange visitor.

I was sitting in the front room with my husband, having a chat and enjoying a cup of tea when I got a strange urge to look at the television set. It appeared as if I was watching a scene from a horse race. I could see a man, someone strange who I had never seen before. He was quite slight and had a gold band with coins hanging from it, wrapped around his head. "Who are you?" I asked.

"My name is Jerome and I would like you to watch carefully what I am about to show you" he replied.

With that, he disappeared from view and I felt my gaze drawn to a new scene that had materialised. What I could se I could make little sense of. Before me, a carnival had appeared. There was a blue sky background; sawdust on the ground and tents reaching up to great heights. How puzzling, I thought, and described what I could see to Joe who could deduce little from it either.

This continued for a few more moments and then it was taken from my sight. Jerome re-appeared in the centre of the room. I was very confused by all this and was about to ask him what he really wanted when I was stopped by the 'phone ringing. It was Meg. Her horse was running in a race that afternoon and she was asking again what it's chances were. I thought about what I had seen for a moment and realised that all that had happened must have been some clue as to who would win the race. I knew it would not be Meg's horse that would win, and so I asked her to look at the race listing and see if there was a horse with 'Carnival' in the name.

When Meg returned with the listings, she confirmed that there was a horse running called Carnival Air and it was an outsider. I told her that this was the winning horse and she should back it. Meg was pleased by this since she was in desperate need of money at the time and her last resort was to place a bet with her bill money so she had wanted to make sure she did not waste it. I asked Meg to call after the race and let me know what happened.

Jerome was still there with a beaming smile on his face and I know he was sent to help Meg.

That evening, Meg called around to see me. I was expecting her to be very happy, having won so much money, but instead, she looked terrible and in need of a good stiff drink. I invited her in and offered her a glass of wine. "What happened?" I asked. Meg went on to explain how she had gone to see her niece before she placed her bet. She had got talking to her and her boyfriend about the bet and told them about the horse that I had predicted would win. When her boyfriend had heard about it he pronounced that it didn't have a hope in hells chance of winning. Rather foolishly, she had listened to him rather than me and decided as such to put all her bill money on her own horse.

She had then returned to her niece's home to watch the race there and was horrified to see Carnival Air take the race with no trouble at all. Meg had lost a fortune by not following Jerome's advice. Needless to say, her niece's boyfriend made a rather hasty departure when the race had finished, as he probably feared for his life! Meg never asked for any information on her horse or other races again.
I still see Jerome from time to time and occasionally, he has suggested horses that I could win a little something on. Not to make a fortune, mind you, more to prove a point. Sometimes, when I am giving help to someone, he appears, and I always able to say when I see him that it is lucky and that things are going to be alright.

****

My gift can also be used to find missing things, both people and objects. There have been numerous occasions where I have been asked to participate in all kinds of searches: missing people; artefacts of historical importance, even animals. It is the story of one of these such animals that I would like to share with you now.
Bertie the cat was missing for 246 days in all. The reason I have chosen to write about Bertie is because his story is very unusual and quite a touching tale of how we should never give up hope when all seems lost because things will always be alright in the end. The catastrophe of the missing cat was brought to my attention because of another cat that I had lead its owner to. The Psychic Press had printed the story of this re-unification and one of their readers, who was aware of Bertie's disappearance, saw the story. A 'phone call was immediately made to Bertie's owners suggesting I may be able to lead them to him.

And so they wrote to the Psychic News to ask them if it was possible to pass on a letter to me, which inevitably they did. Upon receipt of the letter, I telephoned Bertie's owners, Ruth and Linda. I had been shown a cat in spirit but I explained to them this was not Bertie and that he was still alive. I then described to them how Bertie had been snatched from under their noses and that he was being held somewhere dark. He was very restricted as to where he could move to and could not break free. I told them that they would have him back in their arms one day, but his leg would have been injured. Most of all though, I stressed that his return would only be possible if they kept looking. I advised them to scour the area; pester the neighbours, and suggested they back track their movements of the day Bertie disappeared. This is what Ruth and Linda had to say about it all.

24th September 1995

Dear Tress,

We cannot begin to express the joy that we feel to have Bertie home again - and we owe most of it to you for giving us hope and for providing us with vital clues. It took us some time to put all of the clues into place, but the wait was certainly worthwhile and we bless the day you decided that you could help us and made that initial telephone call in response to our letter. So - now for the full facts.

Bertie is our wonder boy

In 1991, we set out to find a boy kitten in an attempt to encourage our lovely tabby cat Katie to develop a will to live; her twin Freddie had recently died. She had brought Freddie up after they had been abandoned by their mother, but when Freddie died aged 8 months, Katie's health began to deteriorate - she needed a baby to take care of. This is when we found our Bertie who was only eight weeks old. From the first moment the two cats met, Katie loved him, and Bertie fell hopelessly in love in return.

Bertie soon became a character in the area . It first began when he carried home a plastic bag full of money; after visiting neighbours we eventually discovered that he had entered their cat flap, grabbed the bag from an inside window sill - and run; the gift of money was followed by a bag of marshmallows, a pack of sandwiches, a note for the P. E. teacher and a pair of black Y- fronts; a bag of potatoes, a leg of lamb and whole salmon! Many of these heavy items were carried through the cat flap and across the kitchen floor. We began to think that we could go into business with an original "cat burglar"!

In spite of his reputation as the best cat-burglar in town, Bertie did manage to survive! He became the most handsome cat in North Yorkshire and proceeded to wipe the board clean at every CPL photographic competition as the "most handsome male", "Judges favourite" and "the best in cat in the show"!

However, none of this was as important as the fact that Bertie has the most wonderful, loving nature and since the moment we first laid eyes on him he became, with Katie, the centre of our lives. Needless to say, our lives were turned completely upside down when we thought that we had lost him --

On the 18th of January 1995, Bertie went out just before his supper, he went to sit on next doors rockery at the end of our drive - it was 8.30pm; by 9.00pm he had disappeared. He would never have left home of his own accord - we were convinced he had been taken.

From then on we hardly slept. We searched every square inch of the neighbourhood; we delivered over 2000 leaflets by hand; notified every vet; every CPL. We spoke to the radio stations, posties, paperboys- the lot! We put up notices on every village board and shop, and every Parish notice-board within a radius of 10 miles from home. We never stopped looking and we never gave up hope - but it became more and more difficult. After 3 months of constant searching it seemed as though we might never find him - the only thing we were certain of was that somewhere Bertie was still alive.

We followed up every single lead during the next months, sometimes five or six a night. All our weekends and spare time were given over to Bertie hunting. We became tired and felt hopeless - until a lady rang and read to us a story from the Psychic News. That's where you came in Tress. The story made us realise that we needed extra special help. I had been to see a psychic medium five days after Bertie's disappearance, he had been unable to help, but you sounded different - as if you really cared about the people who sought your help and so we decided to write and ask you to contact us.

On Sunday the 23rd of April you told us over the telephone about the spirit of a dark patchy cat with a white nose and feet who was present, he had a problem with his mouth or tongue - this was obviously our Tommy, who had died the year before we adopted Katie and Freddie. You were certain from then on that Bertie was alive - and for this news we thank you. You endorsed what we felt - you gave us hope and the strength to carry on our search.

Over the following weeks you gave us lots of information-

This is what you said:
There were important things to look for like a circle or roundabout; a square of open land with a play area and you could see a large open space at the back of a house which had cattle and sheep nearby, locked in by rough fencing or mesh You also identified the letters E.M.W as being important. You said a lady would be feeding him when we found him and that there was water near to where Bertie would be found. You told us you could see Bertie had a slight injury to his leg. Also that there was a shop and/or business premises with cars parked nearby. There was also something spinning, like a rotary washing line or windmill. You saw a lopsided, disfigured tree and highlighted the importance of an end town house with a narrow opening at it's side.
You saw an open shed or storage building near the house and an archway or bridge. You believed that we would find him in or near a cul-de-sac. You impressed upon us the importance of re-tracing our steps as we had been talking to someone three months after Bertie's disappearance who could help us. You told us that you could see acorns and chestnut trees nearby and a large building with pointed roof, maybe a church. You stated that someone in the house travels a lot and that the numbers 19 and 246 were important, also another cat around Bertie which was black and white.
This is what we found:
A great deal of what you said was an accurate description of the main area at the heart of our village. It was also the description of the village green and turning circle in Newton-On-Ouse where we found Bertie. The letters E. M. and W? Our village playing field is called the Ethel Ward Memorial field !

The lady who eventually took in Bertie when she found him in May was called Elaine Mary and she was a Writer. She lived in front of some farm land used for grazing cattle. Her garden had a rotary washing line in and ran down to the River Ouse (hence the water you described) and the lopsided tree was the topiary garden in the village. As for Bertie's leg, your words were certainly true. He now has arthritis in his back left hip as result of injury while he was away. The house where we found Bertie was an end town house and was next door to the Dawnay Arms in Newton-On-Ouse, with a large car park. The pub was opposite an old barn that had been converted into private garages.

The house was also at the far end of a cul-de-sac and was indeed near the arch of a bridge. True - we had actually gone to the house after a message from a local garage owner - but the lady felt that the cat she had did not match Bertie's description.

As for the acorns and chestnut trees, these could be found on the village green of Newton Church only a few yards away. You can see the spire of this church from miles around. The numbers you mentioned can be accounted for as so. Newton-On-Ouse is across the main A19 trunk road and the number 246 relates to the length of time Bertie was missing for 246 days in all. Oh, and the black and white cat was next door to where Bertie was found and he didn't like Bertie at all!

This is just the tip of an ice-berg of clues you gave us. Some of them, we assume must relate to the area where Bertie was first kept - but we shall probably never know about this, although we have our suspicions. Your willingness to come to our home and walk the area with us certainly made someone panic because it was at that

time that Bertie was taken to Newton and dumped. It was then, thankfully, that Elaine found him and took him in. He was in a reasonable state physically - but a psychological wreck. She cared for him and loved him. I'm sure she was sad to see him go but pleased too that he was reunited with us. We are grateful to her. Our thanks to Alan also since he, independently of yourself, gave much the same information as you and also mentioned the garage and its important link in finding Bertie.
So Tress, these are the details as we matched them up.
Love to Joe and Alan
And of course to Tulsa and Princess!
Take Care
Ruth & Linda.

I'm sure you'll agree that this is a fascinating story, and one with a motto we should never forget - keep your faith alive. It certainly inspired me, and had an effect on others. Some people now know me as the Psychic Pet Detective!

14

Cause And Effect

Every day, our actions can have an effect on the life of another, or cause a specific reaction. We each have a role to play in this life and it is up to each individual how he or she inacts it. Our interactions with others guide us through the present and to the future along the many pathways of right and wrong. We have freedom of choice whichever path we take - sometimes it is the right choice, sometimes not.

As we go through life interacting with each other, we can have a profound effect on other lives. What I would like to illustrate in this chapter is how important it is for us all to treat each other with dignity and respect. Sometimes our actions could push someone down the wrong path with disastrous consequences, so we need to be aware. Take this scenario for example.

There are two children in a playground. One child is quiet and sensitive, whilst the other is the school bully. The bully looks at all the children in the school, deducing who it is that he can safely pick on without repercussions. Bullying weaker children gives him a sense of power and the longer he is allowed to continue, the more he enjoys it. His friends are only so because they live in fear of him. He is not a nice person! As this progresses, he begins to physically hurt the quiet child. Soon the parents of the quiet child notice a significant change in his behaviour. He does not want to go to school and becomes withdrawn and moody. He even starts to play truant. The child fears that if he tells his parents about his trouble then it will make things worse and he will be bullied even more and so he keeps quiet. One day, the quiet child decides that he can no longer go on living like this and takes his own life rather than face the bully day in and day out. He is disoriented, having been thrown into the spirit world before his time and his parents are left devastated with their lives ruined. Yet the bully, with no remorse at all, continues to manipulate others throughout his life, pushing those he encounters down sombre and depressing pathways - this is cause and effect (albeit and extreme example).

It can go beyond this. Suppose the quiet child was meant to marry and have children. One of those children was meant to become a physician who made a tremendous discovery that aided mankind. Not now. All because of the actions of one person.

That bully, however, had he been stopped from behaving so badly, could have become a very positive contributor to society had he realised the error of his ways. Instead, all he can expect when he passes is a very painful life review where he is made to relive all the anguish and suffering that he caused on Earth, as felt and seen through the eyes of the tormented. He has assigned his own place in the afterlife, which would amount to little more than a shack with an overgrown garden, whilst the quiet child who suffered for so long will hold a mansion in comparison. We all have to work out our wrong doings (karma) in the next life, be it in spiritual work or by re-birth to learn from the mistakes we made in the past. Just because we are rich and successful in this world does not mean we can take it with us, if what we have achieved here was at the cost of others.

We all say and do things that can cause another to suffer, but most of the time we apologise and try our best to make up for it. We allow ourselves to get angry and upset and say something we do not mean without thinking of the ramifications. I think most of us can be forgiven for this though, if we can find it in ourselves to admit we were wrong and apologise. By doing this you put in motion the cogs that turn the cause and effect you have caused from wrong to right, even if the results aren't always immediately forthcoming.

There is only one story that I am going to draw upon from personal experience to illustrate all this to you. I have in front of me at this moment in time a picture of a beautiful little baby who is now seven months old, called Paul. His mother Trisha came to me for a reading some time before Paul was born. She was told by spirit that she was going to face a very difficult decision since the father of the unborn child was not ready to accept responsibility of bringing up a child. Their relationship had been a long term one but even so, the father was not ready for this level of commitment and so had issued the "It's the baby or me" ultimatum. All this had been very traumatic for Trisha who loved her boyfriend very much and was torn about whether to sacrifice her baby or keep her man.

It is not for me to pass judgement on anybody, least of all Trisha, and I merely gave to her what spirit had given to me. They wanted her to know that if she went ahead with the pregnancy, then she would have the most beautiful boy in the world to hold in her arms and that he would repay her with love for all the hard times she was going through. Her boyfriend would come round to the idea eventually and would want to get to know his son and spend more time with him. She would never regret having her baby. I made it clear though, that these words were the words of spirit, not a personal viewpoint. Trisha took her reading away with her on tape and played it over and over again. I believe she made the right decision in keeping the baby, which she said the tape helped convince her to do.

The next time I saw Trisha was at my Centre. She had Paul in her arms and she was smiling from ear to ear. Even though he was but a few weeks old, she had brought him to see me. She told me how it had been my strength and the words on the tape that had made her decide to keep Paul. I like to think that this was cause and effect on my part, in the fact that Paul was allowed to come into this world and be given a chance to make a good life for himself and have a family of his own. Had Trisha decided to terminate her pregnancy, who knows how she would have felt now and what pathways she would now be treading?

Very recently, Trisha has been back to see me again and told me that Paul's father now wants access to his son. Just how much cause and effect this will have remains to be seen.

Symbolic View Of Cause And Effect

The seed of life begins within
It is passed on from generation to generation
Like the seasons Spring, Summer, Autumn, Winter
We are like the little flower which pushes its way up through the soil

Spring Of Life

As Spring begins, we rise from the soil
As the season progresses we grow in strength and form and colour

All our needs are taken care of by Mother Nature
We fear nothing, as we feel secure in the soil
It feeds and clothes us
'Till we are strong enough to withstand the storms that will come our way
Or does a tiny weed stunt our growth
Cause us to take a different path; A less secure one
Which robs us of beauty, colour and vital energy

Summer Of Life

As Summer begins, we are at the stage where we begin to open out
As the petals unfold, we enjoy the Sun which warms us
We now begin to share the wealth that we gain from nature
We start to be of service to our surroundings in one form or another
The bee employs us and repays us with what is in abundance to it
Even the weed that can rob us of vital energy in time will have to give back its plunder.

Autumn Of Life

As the Autumn approaches, we begin to wind down
And begin to take what life is left at our leisure
As we sit in the Autumn in the warmth of the fading Sun
We look back over our lives and enjoy what we shared with one another
Have the elements been kind or hurtful to us?
Have we done all we could for each other?
Did we sow that tiny seed when we had the chance?
Or were we too wrapped up in our own survival?

Winter Of Life

As Winter approaches we know that our time above the soil is nearing its end
Our stem is growing weaker, we are losing the strength to stand up in the wind
We begin to feel the cold chill in the air
Do the neighbouring trees and shrubs that surround us give us warmth and shelter in the sleet and snow?
Or do they wrap their leaves around themselves and forget about us?
Or did we help each other as we progress through the seasons of life?
As we lay our heads down in the final moments of life
In the knowledge that we left a tiny seed planted safely in the ground
Waiting for its turn to spring forth and blossom to carry on the cycle of life
Were we selfish or were we robbed of the chance
Did we earn it, or no?

Given to Tress Connor by Sarah, a family member in Spirit

15

My Mother

Some time in June 1995, I had gone to bed looking forward to a good nights sleep. I did not realise it at the time, but this night was to proceed to be the beginning of a very painful and disturbing period in my life; a period that would call on me to give my sister and brothers' a great deal of support, to help them through what was going to be a very difficult time. It was the run up to a point when I would lose something very precious to me. It was a night I will remember for the rest of my life, but it is a memory that I will always be grateful for as it helped us all through the ensuing months. That night I was given a vision.

As I have said earlier in this book, I have always had a fondness for my uncle Dan and would look forward to his visiting me from the spirit world. On this occasion, however, my uncle was to bring me a message about my mother. He and mum kept very much in touch over the years, so it came as no surprise to me that he should be the one to come forward from the spirit world to give me a warning in a vision about my mother.

On numerous occasions my mum would say to me "When it's my time to go you will know. Your uncle Dan will come to you and tell you". She would then add "You know that I love you all and I will look after you when I go". I, in turn, would prepare mum for passing over by telling her about the beautiful place she would be going to and that all her family would be at hand to welcome her home.

I was very much aware in my sleep that I was going to be the bearer of sad tidings as I was taken back in time to old and familiar surroundings. That night, I was taken to the flats at St. Teresas Gardens where we had moved to after the fire on The Coombe. I was watching myself walking down the stairs. When I was nearly at the bottom of the steps I saw Dan step out in front of me, which surprised me as I was not expecting to see him - my first reaction was to say to him "What are you doing here uncle Dan" but I thought better of it and simply said "Hello". I smiled politely as it was nice to see him.

He was standing a short distance away from me and he greeted me with a smile in return. "Where are you going?" he asked as I continued down the last three steps.

"I'm only going around the corner on an errand for mum" I said, passing him at this point.

"Well don't be long. I'm going to see your mother as I've got something to do before I retire. Don't leave it too long, do you hear?" he said quite sternly.

"Yes" I replied "I'll be back in two minutes." I remember thinking it very nice to see my uncle again after all these years and so I hurried away so I could get back to see him before he left.

The next thing I remember seeing was my mother standing in front of me, chatting to a lady I did not recognise. The lady was sitting in an old leather chair that we had while living on the Coombe. The whole atmosphere was charged with memories of my childhood. I was conscious of the fact that my mother looked so young and I was very curious as to who this other lady could be. My mother appeared to know her very well and seemed very excited by the fact that

she had come to visit. I then remembered that uncle Dan was supposed to be there. "Where is uncle Dan? He was coming to see you" I blurted out.
"I haven't seen him" came the reply from my mother. I became concerned as to why he hadn't arrived and told mum that I was going to look for him. Mum kept insisting that he must be somewhere nearby. Dan knew the area very well and it was unlikely that he would have gotten lost. Mum smiled at me and carried on chatting happily to her visitor.
As I set off to look for my uncle, I paused for a moment to think about the chair that the lady had been sitting in, since I recalled it having been reduced to a pile of ashes some time before. It was all very strange.
I resumed my search for my uncle. Within moments I had encountered another face, a young girl with long fair hair. She stepped out of the shadow to confront me and said "You are looking for your uncle. I will take you to him as I know were he is." I instinctively knew that it this face belonged to my daughter, Hayley, who I had mis-carried years before. She took my hand and led me to a stairway that was nearby. I remember thinking to myself that this was a beautiful spiral staircase. It seemed to go on forever and it branched of into every possible direction. "You would never find your way around here on your own" said Hayley, "that is why I have come to guide you." We began to climb the stairs. "We have to turn right at the top if you want to find your uncle."
We seemed to reach some sort of a level, I won't say the top because this staircase expanded everywhere. As we stood on this level, a young boy came forward and took my hand. He used his other hand to point to an opening. "This way" he said, as he led us along a dark corridor that led out onto open greenery.
A short distance away from us, I could see some people. A

man in the group seemed to be giving instructions to the others. "Let's go ask them if they have seen my uncle".
"OK" said the boy. Hayley approached the gentleman and asked if he had seen a man wearing a trilby hat pass by. "Yes" he replied, pointing to a building in the distance. "He's over there". He then looked directly at me and said "But you are not allowed to go there. You're not even supposed to be here. You must go back the way you came, you must go back." Not really sure what was happening, I quickly thanked him and he smiled and turned back to his people. My young friend saw this as an opportunity not to be missed and whispered, "Quick while they're not looking. There is another way. It isn't used very often." We set off in another direction but we were soon spotted and so we hurried ourselves.
We ran straight into a dead end. "Quick, follow me" said the boy.
"But there is a wall there, we can't get out that way" I told him.
"Don't worry, it will break away when you touch it."
I was a little dubious at that prospect, "I'm not like you" I said, "I can't get through that wall!"
"Trust me" said my daughter "it will break away for you and you will be back at the bottom of the stairs where we started."
I plucked up courage and headed for the wall. Low and behold, it just crumpled away at my fingertips as soon as I touched it. I found myself back where we had started. I was very relieved because I knew that somehow I had crossed the forbidden zone - the place we go to when we have passed over. It is here that we account for our lives on Earth and is a place that is further into the spirit world than we are ever intended to go, until we pass. "You can find your own way back from here" said my two chaperons, "we must go now as they'll be looking for us." We waved goodbye.

As I set off back to the flat I was aware that I able to see some of the old places where my old friends had lived. My vision did not seem to be restricted to one dimension - I was "all seeing", like an eagle at a great height. It was quite exhilarating. Then I woke up.

I sat up in bed with a start. Looking over, I saw that it was 3:40am. I tried to make sense of my vision and realised that this was indeed the warning my mother had often foretold of. Dan's last task before he retired into the Forbidden Zone was to warn me of my mother's impending passing. I had already known at the time that my mother was ill, since Alan had visited her a few months before, but I had not realised just how bad she actually was and how rapidly she had deteriorated in such a short time. It became clear that it was my responsibility to prepare the family for the inevitable day. I lay there wondering how I was going to break the news to them. I pondered this for a time, feeling that I would get no more sleep that night.

After a time, as I grew more and more restless, I was relieved to feel a familiar calmness wash over me and the sound of a trusted voice ring through my ears. "Don't worry, we will help you." It was my grandmother, coming to offer her support as she had done so many times before. I hardly seemed to think of anything else and found myself drifting off into a peaceful sleep.

The next morning, I told Joe all about my vision, saying I would ring my sister that evening. I knew it would be hardest to tell Clare as she is quite ill herself and is confined to a wheelchair most of the day. She is a very sensitive lady but somehow I knew that she would be able to handle it.

True to form, I called my sister that evening to tell her that I had a visit from uncle Dan. She informed me that she had been saying to her husband Brian for a few days that she felt all was not well with mum. I was glad that she sensed this for herself because it meant that my call was not proving to be as big a blow as I had anticipated. It also paved the way for my next words as I told her that our brother Joseph, who looked after our mother in Ireland, was keeping a lot of information back from us because he felt that we might not handle it very well. I knew he was having a tough time himself and that he must be bottling an awful lot up inside himself. He, most of all, despite seeing her condition, seemed the one who did not want to let her go. I advised Clare to go see mum, and help to give our brother a little break since things were going to get much, much worse. He was very close to mother and took very good care of her in her later years.

The next step was to prepare my younger brother, Seamus. I called him but he was out at the time so I left a message with his wife asking him to contact me as soon as possible. When he did return my call, I told him very much what I had told Clare "Go see mum while you still can". They decided to space their visits apart slightly so as not to alarm our mother. True to my vision, the warning had indeed been accurate for my mother was very ill. When they arrived in Ireland and saw mum, she was in a very bad way and had to be given constant care and attention by my eldest brother. He was continually having to ferry mum from one hospital to another. He was very highly strung and in need of a break so having Clare and Seamus over there helped lift my mothers spirits and eased the burden on him somewhat, if only for a short while.

Whilst they were there, they were able to observe how mother was beginning to see spirit more and more of the time and they used this as an opening to tell her that I had seen our uncle Dan and that I had suggested that they go. I think she knew that her time was short because she did not seem duly alarmed by this. She had even commented to Alan a few months before that her time was running out and she was "Not long for this world. Thank God" I think it must have been a relief for her because she was suffering so much with so many different ailments.

As time moved on, I was receiving messages from my family in spirit that mum was getting closer to her time and so I was never shocked to hear that she had been taken back into hospital. This went on right up until the end of October, when mum asked to be admitted to a hospice. By now she had to be constantly nursed at home and could no longer look after herself. My mother was always very stubborn about letting people do things for her as she was extremely independent, and right up to the very last moment I know she would have tried to keep that dignity but it seemed that even that now was too much. We weren't very happy about her going into a hospice since we knew that she would give up on life once she was admitted so, despite her request, we talked her out of it. Instead she was admitted into hospital. Here she was administered morphine injections regularly throughout the day to blot out her pain. I was happier knowing that she was being constantly monitored and that I could at least keep tabs on her progress, since I always knew when something had happened and was able to phone the hospital for updates.

On the night of Tuesday the 7th of November, I received another visit from uncle Dan who told me that I should prepare the family for mother's passing since it was very close now. It was a very difficult time to concentrate on anything else and I found myself distracted. I hold a development group on Wednesday evenings and I admit it was a burden this particular night. I was just glad that it was the last session for a few weeks so that I could put my mind onto family matters. Before we parted though, I advised the circle that it would be the last time we would meet whilst my mother was still alive and that she would pass next Tuesday. As soon as I got in that night I called my sister and brother and told them that if they wanted to say "Goodbye" to mum, they would have to go now. My sister took this very well and was grateful for the warning. She decided to go over on the Tuesday morning since it was the earliest time she could get over. I sent her down some photos of my family which is what mother had requested from me through Joseph. Clare had already bought a special blanket, which my mother had also asked me for which I asked her to take over. I also wrote mum the last letter she would receive from me. I wanted to make sure she had everything she wanted before she passed. The Sunday night was very touch and go for her. She had to be revived twice during the night and had received the last rites. We did not think she was going to make it, but thankfully she was able to hold on just a little bit longer; it wasn't her time yet. This was the one time through it all that I wished I could have jumped on a plane and been with her physically, even though I was always there spiritually. It was a very distressing night. I think that part of the reason she held on was that she knew she was going to see her children one last time, since the hospital had told her of their intentions to fly over.

On Monday morning, mother insisted that she be transferred to a hospice. She desperately wanted to be in a place where there were nuns, and so this time, her wishes were complied with. She was moved that same afternoon.

Tuesday the 14th of November was a terrible day for us all. Alan arranged for some flowers to be delivered from her and made plans to fly over. Meanwhile, my sister and brother

were sat by her bedside. She was given the blanket and photos that she had asked for and my letter was read out to her. She also received the flowers that had been sent. At 8 o'clock that night, my mother let go of this world.
By 9 o'clock, every pain I had taken from my mother and transferred to myself to try and ease her suffering, was lifted from me. I knew my mother's spirit was set free from the chains of life that had bound her.
Mum came through to Alan first before anybody. What he was able to describe to me was that my mother was overflowing with feelings of relief and happiness. Her suffering was over and the healing could now begin. When she first reached out to Alan, he had been looking for a specific photo that he had of him and his Nan. The picture was buried within a pile of other photos but, he simply put his hand into the pile and pulled out that one photo - first time! She then came through to me, and has done so many times since. I think it proper for me to let her tell you in her own words exactly what the whole experience was like.

New Dawn

As I walked through the garden of my Father's kingdom
I stood in awesome wonder at the sights there are within
The children at the lily pond full of laughter, I could see
The guides were all around them wearing sashes of green and blue
With long white flowing robes and on their feet were slippers of gold
I sat beneath the Tree Of life; It's branches bowing down
To welcome me to a bright new shining dawn
Both my parent's right here with me, my husband by my side

And in the distance not far from me, my brothers and sisters I could see
And what a sight that was that filled my heart indeed
As I slowly walked to greet them, still fairly weak it seems
What joy welled up inside me all but brought me to my knees
Oh what a grand time I was having; my soul at last was free
From all the pain and sorrow that in life surrounded me
My thoughts still for my children I asked that I may see
In life were scattered some near some far from me
For the last thing I remember as I sent two off for tea
For the whole day they had been sitting so very close to me
One was my youngest daughter, the other my closest son
Beneath my hands were photos of my eldest daughter, her husband and their son
The blanket I had asked for, was pressed up to my lips
Then placed across my chest
All was given that I'd asked for and was a final request from me
For upliftment it did bring me; It helped to set me free
All the pain and suffering it began to drift away
And I looked up to see my mother standing looking down at me
My father stood beside her, his hand extending outwards to me
He gently called to me
"It is time to go my daughter to pastures green and bright"
"It's time to start your journey. We must guide you to the light"
All my timing was just right; not a single child of mine in sight
I best go quickly now and I wished with all my might
That mercy and goodness follow throughout all my

children's lives
As the last breath drifted from me, I began to float away
My mother took my hand in hers and so gently spoke to me
"Let's journey a little further and show you all that you may wish to see"
"Let's go and see the others" came a voice from deep within me
But no words out loud were spoken, no movement of lips could I feel
And yet those words were spoken and clearly said by me
With their arms around me carrying, mother and father by my side
No plane, no boat was needed; None was necessary for me
I was at my daughters bedside. My will and spirit free
And as I stood there smiling, my daughter said to me
"Mother will you tell me why it's so hard for you to leave"
"I know you are not frightened as you were so well prepared"
As I bent to stroke her forehead I answered with these words
"I will not tell, I'll show you the reason I was afraid to go"
I brought all emotion up within her from far deep down below
The pain the hurt and sorrow I knew would surely follow
When I did lose my mother I felt hurt I'd never known
She understood the facts so clearly; The truth I had made known
"Oh mum", I heard her say to me "I'm truely glad to say"
I would not want this sorrow on any waking day
I placed my lips upon her cheek then gave a gentle wave
As she smiled back at me, and I grateful for the moment
That we both had shared together
My time allowed was over, but I still visit her each day

I made a promise to all my children
I told them in many a way
That I will be beside you
And watch over you all the way
Until we meet in God's green land again - I am looking towards that day
But until such times draw near; I am never far, I'm always near.

I was inspired to write these words by my mother, God rest her soul. She truely was a gift to this world, like so many mothers who have come and gone before.

****

As for the future, what does it hold for me? Well, my work is sure to continue through healing and consultations. I've had many invitations to travel abroad to such places as America, Germany and Spain to demonstrate my mediumship and healing.

1997 has been a hectic year. A year in which my primary goal has been to see this book out there with you. But so much else has happened in the time after my mothers' passing, that I have already begun to compile a selection of stories for my second book.

I hope that the writings in this book, however, go some of the way to showing the world, and more importantly, science, that there is a whole other world out there just waiting for us. We may not be able to examine or analyse it, but it is there and it's there for all of us, believer or not.

So, until we meet again, please remember;

The Best Is Yet To Come

TESTIMONIALS

Five Original Letters Of Support

Here is a letter I received from a lady who I have come to know very well in the last three years. The first time we met I gave her some healing on her leg and foot as I had picked up that she had hurt it very badly in some way, as a result of some kind of accident, which had happened some years before. She confirmed this after the healing session was finished. Sometime later, she contacted me again to ask me if I could help her with some more healing. I will let her tell you in her own words (name and address changed).

De,
Cookridge,
Leeds
West Yorkshire.
28th of October 1992

Dear Tress,

Should you ever need a testimonial the following should certainly count as such.

When I first met you I had been undergoing treatment as an outpatient at a local hospital for one year. A few weeks later my condition suddenly worsened and I had to be admitted to hospital urgently and underwent a major operation. The operation was expertly carried

out, and for that I am grateful.
However due to the healing I received through you soon afterwards I made a swifter recovery than I had been led to expect. In addition each time subsequently that I have had a check-up the consultant had commented on how well the tissue had healed.
Some time later a similar condition arose in a another area. This time the consultant decided to operate immediately. However, due to the general lack of resources I was not called for. By this time I had been receiving healing from you regularly, and the condition had gradually disappeared.
When I was finally called for an operation I insisted on having an outpatient examination. The consultant, accompanied by a student, could find nothing wrong, I explained that this had come about thanks to the spiritual healing I had received from you. The atmosphere cooled distinctly, which was sad, but I had made an important point. An x-ray was organised, but it was clear.
I returned for a check up six months later, and again all was clear. So I have been spared not only from a second operation, but from extensive convalesce, and a consequent total loss of earnings, as I am self employed.
For this I am more grateful than I can say to you Tress, and to the spirit world .

with love and thanks from De

Mrs. Alchorne first came to me for a reading in the late summer of 95, and as the reading was coming to a close I was inspired by spirit to look towards her swollen hand. I felt that I could help her by giving her spiritual healing. So in my usual tactful way asked what the problem was and she briefly informed me of the circumstances. I only gave her a few seconds of healing, as I was told by spirit that was all it would take. From this point on I will let Mrs. Alchorne tell you in her own words. The address has been changed to protect Mrs. Alchorne.

Mrs. P. Alchorne
20 Ferry Hill
Leeds

Dear Tress
For some time now I have been meaning to write to you primarily to try put into words how grateful I am that I came to you for a reading. At that time I had no knowledge that you were also a healer. After a most impressive and relaxed reading, you noticed that my right hand was swollen and asked me what the problem was and I then briefly told you the circumstances.
To put into perspective and, hopefully, to help others who may have experienced the indifference and scepticism of some members of the medical fraternity, I give below a not so brief summary of what happened to me and ultimately the outcome .
In June 1992, I was employed as a telephone operator using a computerised system and working to strict timings. I began to suffer severe pains in my knuckles and wrist of my right hand which affected my speed of handling and I was referred to the company doctor. He immediately diagnosed that I had arthritis and put me on sick leave. I saw him again some four weeks later and then began a course of physiotherapy which lasted for six months with no improvement whatsoever. He then referred me to the Rheumatology Dept., at St.

James' Hospital where I had many x-rays, nerve conduction tests, cortisone injections under my knuckles and into my wrists and, although the tests were inconclusive, all the doctors stated that I did have arthritis. I disputed this as no other part of my body was affected but they dismissed the idea out of hand.

I was then referred to a specialist in work related injury and he stated that my hand injury could have been caused by working on a computer but this was very hard to prove. I saw him again a year later but he could not categorically say what was wrong. I was, through all this, on various drugs which were of no use at all. In July, 1993, I was retired from work on medical grounds. During the courses of treatment I was given many drugs which did no good at all and, in 1995, further tests were given and the final blood tests revealed that I did not have arthritis. I do not have to return to hospital until June, 1996.

Up to and after my last visit to hospital, I could not use my hand properly. I could not write well, garden, grip anything tightly, or do any of the things which I had previously taken for granted. I had come to terms with it and learned to live with it and then, I came to you for a reading and the unthinkable happened. You placed my hand between yours and I felt an immense heat and pins and needles all over. This lasted for less than a minute and, from that day to this, I have never had another pain or twinge of any kind and can use my hand normally again.

When I next visited my GP I told him what had happened and he tested my grip and flexibility of movement and was amazed. He was delighted about what the outcome of my visit to you had been and

thoroughly approved.
Thank you again Tress from the bottom of my heart. If this letter can be of any help in dispelling other people's fears or doubts about the God given gift of spiritual healing which you have, you have my full permission to use any part, or all, of it. My visit to you brought a change in my lifestyle which I thought had gone forever.

Sincerely,
Mrs. P. Alchorne.

This is a letter I received regarding a recent postal reading that I completed for a lady called Julie of Flexion in Manchester. She had sent me a sample of handwriting and a photograph along with a brief letter asking a few general questions.
It is nice to receive feedback on postal readings as the sitter is not in the room with the medium. I have to trust in the spirit world with whatever information comes through. I think postal readings offer wonderful proof that there is a force at work outside of our material world. I will let Julie tell you in her own words what she made of her postal reading.

Julie
Flixton
Manchester
9th August 1995

Dear Tress,
I hope this short note finds you well. I am writing to confirm the information you gave on the tape.
At the beginning of the tape you mentioned that there was cancer in the family my mother had breast cancer thirteen years ago, you mentioned that my grandmother and grandfather are both in spirit, which is correct.

You gave me the name Ivy who was my grandmothers sister who is also in spirit.
The Roman Catholic link comes from my grandmother, so does the Irish link you mentioned.
Someone around you linked to drama/TV - my friend works at the BBC in Manchester.
The year 1967 you mentioned was the year I was born.
The stroke and coma condition was my uncle who is also in spirit.
You were right when you said that there has been many emotional set backs and bereavements in my family over the last twelve years.
You mentioned that something happened five weeks ago - separation from my friend Jennifer.
You picked from the Elaine photograph that someone who is doing some D.I.Y. is her boyfriend Tony.
The cancer condition around her was her husband Tony who passed away. The person who passed over suddenly and tragically with a condition affecting the head was Elaine - Who passed over with a brain haemorrhage.
There were two house moves around Elaine and you were correct in saying that one of the house moves was a distance away from Manchester to Oswestry.
You were also correct when you said that the link between Elaine and I was spiritual, the February month you mentioned is the month in which Elaine passed away.
From the hand writing I sent you - you were correct when you said that Jennifer lives somewhere where there are open fields and horses are kept in the adjoining fields. Jennifer is linked to flowers. She was my floristry tutor. The J around her is her sister and the name Betty is her mothers name. You picked up a lot of countries

connected to Jennifer; she enjoys travelling abroad. You were also correct in saying that she is ,an animal lover. My energy levels are very low and I would be grateful if you could give me Spiritual healing. Do I have to ring the number you gave me to make an appointment for healing?
Lastly I want to thank you Tress for the reading you gave me, I was very pleased with it.

God bless you
Julie

This testimonial is from a lady in Ireland that requested a postal reading. People write to me for all kinds of different reasons but this reading was requested due to bereavement. I have never met the lady in person, but she had heard of me through a relative of hers who has received spiritual healing from me. When a postal reading takes place, in most cases, the spiritual medium has had no contact at all with the individual prior to the letter requesting the reading. Therefore, it can be said that contact on a spiritual level is relied upon. I have left her families first and surnames out in order to protect them as they live in a close community. So in her own words I will let this lady, whom I shall call Nan, tell her own story.

NAN
Sligo
Ireland

Dear Tress,

Many thanks for your reading on tape which you sent to me. I am sorry for not having written earlier to you but I needed to listen to it several times. I have to say I found it fascinating and accurate in everything you said. I did not understand the relevance of several points, but they may become clearer as time passes. It has given me great comfort and hope for the future because as you rightly said I have kept a lot bottled up inside.

I will now try to go through your tape, one point at a time and make any comments I feel is necessary. (1) You have confirmed what I originally felt about having the house put into joint names. (2) I feel very guilty about the fact that dad gave us money but he did insist (and used the word gift as you done) that it was a gift not to be repaid. He stated that he was entitled to give anything to whoever he wished. My husband and I will continue to be very grateful to him. (3) You have repeated exactly what the consultant and my counsellor have said as regards a family problem that it will take time. It has improved in the last two weeks. (4) A lot of cancer in family my husbands grandfather, my mother, my father, and paternal uncle passed from cancer. (5) Lily, my husbands grandmother: John, my husbands grandfather; Pat, maternal granduncle. September is my father-in-laws birthday. The letter 'D' could be my Aunt Dorothy who has been difficult at times. (6) My daughter had a dog that was brown black and white which she loved. Another dog belonging to my late uncle. (7) You mentioned the name Budgie, my husband's grandfather was called Budgie as a pet name and this would only have been known to very few close relatives. (8) My grandfather always carried a walking stick with a gold handle. (9) Dad always wore a trilby hat and the children have both been wearing it lately in play. (10) My daughter is very artistic paints and plays piano. (11) Yes, I have cried inwardly long and hard and yes I do a very low self-esteem. (12) Two Mary's - my mother and sister who, although called Louise, was christened Mary. (13) Stamps - and there is a very valuable selection which we have had valued by expert in Dublin. (14) You mentioned two wedding rings. I wear two rings and have done since my mother died seventeen years ago. (15) My husband does miss his grandparents terribly for he did spend many holidays with them (yes they left a large gap in his life) and he has often said that had his grandparents been here he would not have failed his exams in collage. (16) Yes I think it is a good marriage too and we do care deeply for one another. (17) Your description of my husband's grandmother could not be more accurate, particularly when you described the aura around her. She was a person that did not sweep anything under the carpet. She was very close to my husband. (18) You mentioned an unexpected journey - could that have been a christening in Dublin we only heard of it the week beforehand. (19) New friend since last October. (20) Constant worry over finances by me. (21) Yes, great disappointment during last three years. (21) You described and used correct title of paternal grand aunt (Aunt Annie). I never knew her but was told she was a very austere woman. (22) Someone very stubborn and selfish at times could it be my aunt in Dublin who I visit every six weeks or so but who did not want any outside help of any kind. She finds it difficult to cope on her own. (23) Yes I have felt like piggy in the middle in family dealings and I was pulled in several directions at the same time. (24) I have mislaid items particularly keys. (25) I have hidden a lot over the last nine or ten years. Yes. Yes. Yes. (26) I know I have creative abilities which have not been utilised properly but in last two months or so I have made some curtains and have redone flower beds in my garden (gardening is one of my hobbies). (27) I do dream of Mum and Dad (Dad did often say the Irish proverbs, sometimes in jest I think). I do hope this is of help to you Tress.

Again many thanks
NAN

This is a copy of a letter I received from a lady I've come to know very well. I thought it might offer comfort if you have ever considered having Spiritual healing. This lady read an article in a magazine and decided that she would write to them as one who had seen the results from spiritual healing for herself. I've changed the name of the person concerned so as to protect her.

Mrs. S. Grand.
Middlesex

Dear Sir or Madam,
With reference to your article in your magazine dated May the 24th 1992, headed "After life is death really the end". I have been healed both mentally and physically by a healer - known as Tress Connor of Leeds, West Yorkshire.
After my mother and a very dear friend died, I felt that everything had fallen apart. I was distraught. Having no other family, Tress and her husband helped me through a very traumatic time, and she would not accept any money for healing. I was told that I could contact them at any time if I needed them.
For fifteen years I had ulcers on my legs as many as four at a time, two ulcers did heal. Tress laid her hands

on them and I was amazed to find that I did not have to wear bandages any more as the ulcers stopped discharging and are completely healed,. Until I met Tress it seemed I was destined to have ulcers on my legs for the rest of my life.

A few weeks ago I went to see Tress because I felt that I needed her help. As soon as I entered the room she said "I can feel so much stress and tension I will give you some healing if you wish," Tress also laid her hands on my knee which had been very painful and the pain which I had experienced eased. I did not tell Tress about the painful knee she just knew. Words cannot explain the inner-most peace which Tress has given to me.

I do believe that there is life after death and that power is given to certain chosen people in order that they can heal and help mankind. In my opinion Tress has been given that wonderful power.

Yours Sincerely,
S. Grand (Mrs.)

SPIRITUAL POETRY

Five Poems Given By Spirit

Death

Death is life, life is death
You are dying from the moment you are born
You come into this world with nothing, you leave with nothing
Your spirit is the real you, not your body
You are spirit with a body, not a body with a spirit
You come from the spirit world & go back to the spirit world
Ashes to ashes, dust to dust, but soul forever.

Forgiveness

Did I leave something undone
Did I leave something unsaid
Why is my heart so painful
With every step I tread

I cared not for the ways of sorrow
I looked to only beg steal or borrow
Take from all to sack and plunder
Forsaking all is it any wonder

How my heart can find no shelter
To separate the bonds that bind me
For in my blindness I was weak
I cared not to even seek

The riches on me that God bestowed
Not one seed I ever sowed
Rock upon rock I boldly laid
Not once did I ever lift a spade

But God in His wisdom took my hand
And showed to me a wonderful land
I prayed and prayed I might be saved
And He plucked me from this dismal grave.

Given to Tress by a young man in spirit called Mick.

Our A. B. C's

A is you being answerable for your own actions
B is you believing in yourself when others put you down
C is you caring for the world and all within it
D is doing for others as you would have others do unto you
E is evolving through your own efforts not through the efforts of others
F is fulfilling your own needs and helping others to fulfil theirs
G is being grateful for help when someone lends a helping hand
H is you helping those less fortunate than yourself
I is insuring you do not injure other souls intentionally
J is being just in all ways both to yourself and to others

K is being kind for the sake of kindness itself
L is living right - love yourself then you will be able to give love
M is making do with what you have and not making another's belongings your own
N is not letting go when all around you has failed
O is not being oppressed when others suppress you
P is to find peace within yourself and instil it in others
Q is to query your thoughts and actions at all times
R is putting right the wrong you may have done by whatever means you can and rising above the wrong done to you
S is strength in your own convictions and to allow others strength in theirs
T is to try - if at first you don't succeed try again for in trying you will not have failed
U is to understand that you are spirit within a body and have free will in all you do and say
V is to value other's principles as you would have them value yours and to value another's life as you value your own
W is for wisdom not only in a worldly sense but in a spiritual sense as well, seek within and you will find wisdom is simplicity itself
X is a way of expressing the love that we have for those that we love and cherish in our lives
Y is for young in heart and in mind for in your heart and mind you remain young for this is the essence of your spirit
Z is for zest in all things, for all is spirit and spirit giving have a zest for life, not only your own but all other and you will truly grow in the ways of the spirit, onward forward and upwards towards the light.

The Plan

Little by little and day by day
In love we send your way
Much tender loving care for all
We have not time to play

For in God's land here much is planned
To stave off pain and sorrow
Worldly goods and falsehoods
Man has pilled upon its shores

To lock it up and bind it not caring
For its well being or even for its faith
But there are some among you
Its surely right to say

That strive to make it safer
So the young can have their day
So ask God in your quietness
To send upon its way

The pearls of understanding
To fill the hearts of man
So peace can come around you
For you are part of God's great plan

Heavens

Watch a moonbeam watch it shine
In its light it is sublime
Casting silver beams of light
Just to brighten up your night
Overflows upon your world

See its silver rays unwind
To lift men's hearts it will unbind

Watch the seas and rivers flow
When tides turn back what they will show
Upon the sands there's much to know
Many things to all of value
Search the shores and search them well
For on and in many things do dwell

Watch the stars that shine at night
Watch their little twinkling light
Like millions of lightbulbs burning bright
Take the time to stop and stare
To see what's happening way out there

Take the time to dwell on things
And what knowledge with it brings
That God's abundant in all things

Given to Tress by Gwen - a friend in spirit
God bless all mankind Gwen

PSYCHIC WORKBOOK

Exercises In Self Healing

Exercise One: Balancing The Chakra

This is a term that means grounding yourself or levelling your energies. It is a simple little exercise which you can use when you are feeling out of sorts, or when it seems as if nothing you have done throughout the day has gone right. You know the type of day, when you do silly things like putting the sugar in the tea pot and the cat in the bath instead of the dog! We have all done silly things like this at some time or another. Some people would say that they have left their spirit in bed when they left home for work - by now you will have got the gist of what I mean. There are six simple steps to help you get through a day like this. As I take you through each step, imagine that there are two cogs or wheels, one rotates clockwise the other anti-clockwise, so that they slot into one another. When you are out of balance these two wheels are working against each other, for example both may be rotating clockwise, or there may be two or more points that may be out of alignment. In simple terms it means you are out of balance. Try this simple meditation for yourself and see how easy it is. Good luck.
Make sure you are sitting comfortably in an upright chair and are not going to be disturbed. This is how to balance

your chakras. Make sure you read through the exercise a few times before you go on in order to clearly understand the procedure. In time you should become a dab hand at it!

The First Step

Raise your hand up just above the top of your head. You can use either hand. Now gently let it rest on top of your head for a few moments. You can close your eyes as you concentrate on the top of your head. Just let the energy flow through your hand down to the chakra.

The Second Step

Bring your hand down to your forehead and let the palm rest right across it. Close your eyes and leave it there for a few moments. This should begin to help you focus better. Two or three minutes should be enough for this.

The Third Step

Bring your hand down to the base of your throat. Put the tips of your fingers across the hollow part (just below the Adam's Apple for the men). Let it rest there and close your eyes. Relax for a few moments before you open your eyes again.

The Fourth Step

Move your hand down to the left-hand side of the chest. This is the area where your heart is. Place your hand across it and close your eyes again. Relax and wait for a few moments as before, and then move on.

The Fifth Step

Bring your hand down to the stomach area at the base of your ribcage and let it rest across it. Close your eyes for a few moments and relax. By now you should be feeling quite loose and calm.

The Final Step

Move your hand down to your waist. Close your eyes and let your hand rest there for a few moments and relax. Open your eyes, take a deep breath and then let it out slowly.

You have now finished levelling your energies and your chakras are balanced. You should now begin to feel lighter within and more focused.

Exercise Two: Self Healing

This is a form of self healing that you can use in the quietness of your own home. It is not advisable to do this whilst you are driving or operating machinery, it is meant to be used in secure surroundings in order that you may take full advantage of it. Make sure that you are not going to be disturbed as you will be meditating. At first, you may find it hard to concentrate or to see the colour that you are trying to visualise, but with a little practice you will soon get the hang of it and find that you are able to bring the colours into focus more easily. You will feel much more calm and relaxed. At the end of your meditation, you will feel more refreshed than you sometimes feel after a nights sleep, even though you have only been meditating for a few minutes.
The eleven colours you will be using will follow on from one another, the first being red, then orange, yellow, pale green, blue, purple, pink, dark green, gold, silver and finally white. Each colour corresponds to a specific part of the body, so please study the diagram and exercise before you start.

Starting The Exercise

Ensure that you are sitting comfortably on an upright chair as this will help you to concentrate better and stop you from falling asleep.

The Colour Red

Close your eyes and imagine that you can see the base of the spine in your mind's eye. Concentrate on this for a few moments and visualise a deep red colour. Imagine a piece of red silk wide enough to cover the whole of your back. Now draw it up the length of your spine, right to the base of your neck. Hold the thought for a couple of minutes and draw energy from the colour, then slowly let the colour fade away.

The Colour Orange

Visualise your stomach area around the base of your ribcage. See now a piece of orange silk and draw it up to your shoulders. Hold it there for a few moments and feel the waves of relaxation wash through you. Slowly let the colour fade away as if the silk was falling into your lap.

The Colour Yellow

Your spleen is found on the left side of the body under your ribcage. Visualise the colour yellow across the ribcage to your waistline. Hold it there for a short time and let it fade away.

The Colour Green

This colour is associated with the chest area. Imagine your piece of silk to be pale green in colour and pull it up to the base of your throat over the whole chest area right out to the edge of your arms. Hold it there as before, then let it gently fade away.

The Colour Blue
The shade of blue you must picture for yourself here is that of the sky. Visualise a short piece of blue silk, like a short scarf, just long enough to encompass the neck. Place it at the back of your throat and bring the colour right up under your chin, wrapping it gently around the whole neck until it meets at the centre. Hold it there, then let it fade away.

The Colour Purple
This colour will cover the third eye, which is in the centre of your forehead. When you have positioned it there, imagine drawing the colour up to the top of your head (the crown). Hold it there for a few seconds. Now add the colour pink to the trail you have created. Leave these colours here as we move on.

The Colour Dark Green
The type of green I refer to at this point is nature's green. It is seen in leaves on the trees during Summer and the grass in the fields. I call it God's colour. Visualise this green in the form of a handkerchief and let it cover the top of your head. Leave it there with the other colours as we move on.

The Colours Gold, Silver And White
Imagine a piece of gold silk, and place it over the green. Let it rest there. Now visualise the colour silver laying on top of the gold. The last colour is white. This is the highest colour of all as it is the purest colour of spirit. Picture this white and allow it to sit on top of the other colours. After a time, allow each colour to slip away, one by one.

When the last colour has faded, allow yourself to open your eyes. You should now feel spiritually cleansed as you have finished your self healing meditation. What you have just done in effect is to give your body a bath from the inside. We take great care to keep our bodies clean on the outside but often forget to cleanse what is within.